THE FIRST PEOPLE

From the earliest primates to Homo sapiens
Where and how our ancestors lived

Devised and produced by
Andrea Dué
Text by
Renzo Rossi

MACMILLAN LIBRARY REFERENCE USA
NEW YORK

INTRODUCTION

First published in Italian by Jaca Book
© Editoriale Jaca Book Spa, Milano
1993

This edition published 1996
by Macmillan Library Reference USA
866 Third Avenue
New York, NY 10022

English Language Translation
Copyright © Simon and Schuster
Macmillan 1996

By Renzo Rossi
Maps by Alessandro Bartolozzi, Roberto
Simoni
Colour illustrations by Giuseppe Cicio,
Claudio Pasqualucci, Rosanna Rea
Black/white illustrations by Andrea Dué,
Roberto Simoni
Translation by Patricia Borlenghi
Edited by Michael Chinery
Scientific adviser Fiorenzo Facchini
Produced by AS Publishing

Library of Congress Cataloging-in-
Publication Data

Rossi, Renzo, 1940-
    [Atlanti della storia dell'uomo.
English]
    The atlas of human history/devised
and produced by Andrea Dué; text by
Renzo Rossi.
        p.; cm.
        Includes indexes.
        Contents: [1] The first people – [2]
The first settlers – [3] Cradles of
civilization – [4] The first Europeans –
[5] Civilizations of Asia – [6]
Civilizations of the Americas.
    ISBN 0-02-860285-4 (v. 1). –
    ISBN 0-02-860286-2 (v. 2). –
    ISBN 0-02-860287-0 (v. 3). –
    ISBN 0-02-860288-9 (v. 4) –
    ISBN 0-02-860289-7 (v. 5). –
    ISBN 0-02-860290-0 (v. 6)
        1. History, Ancient – Maps for
children. 2. Historical geography –
Maps for children. 3. Children's atlases.
[1. Civilization, Ancient – Maps.
2. Historical geography – Maps.
3. Atlases.]
    I. Dué, Andrea. II. Title.
G1033.R6 1996 <G&M>
930–dc20   95-8622
                                      CIP
                                  MAP AC

Printed and bound in Italy by Grafiche
Editoriali Padane Spa, Cremona

An Atlas tells you about history in a way that a history book alone cannot. *The Atlas of Human History* maps the course of human history on a journey that began about four million years ago. At that time, and during subsequent periods of history, the world was not as it is today. We know now that the continents are continually moving, slowly inching together in one place and apart in another. When the first humanlike creatures evolved from their primate ancestors, Europe and North America were joined together but separated from Africa where the oldest pre-human fossils have been found. When sea-levels dropped, a land bridge emerged, allowing our pre-human ancestors to cross into Eurasia from Africa.

All living things are tied to their environment. How they live depends on where they live. Today, we can to an extent change the conditions in which we live. We can heat our homes if we live in cold climates, cool them if we live in hot places. The earliest people could not change the world around them; they had to adapt to it or die. Eventually they made discoveries and developed skills that allowed them to change their environment. They used fire and tools, and began to live as humans, developing language, artistic skills and spiritual awareness, and living together in communities.

The First People traces the origins and developments of *Homo sapiens* and earlier pre-human species. Successive maps chart the spread of humans from Africa to other continents, as people moved from place to place to take advantage of more favourable conditions where food was easier to find.

Later titles in the series describe how and where prehistoric peoples settled and founded villages and towns. From them grew the great civilizations of the ancient world and the later civilizations of the New World. Seeing where people lived and understanding the nature of the place and its climate gives us a fresh insight into history.

M.C.

CONTENTS

1 THE ORIGIN AND EVOLUTION OF LIFE

The numbers indicate the time since the beginning of each period, in millions of years.

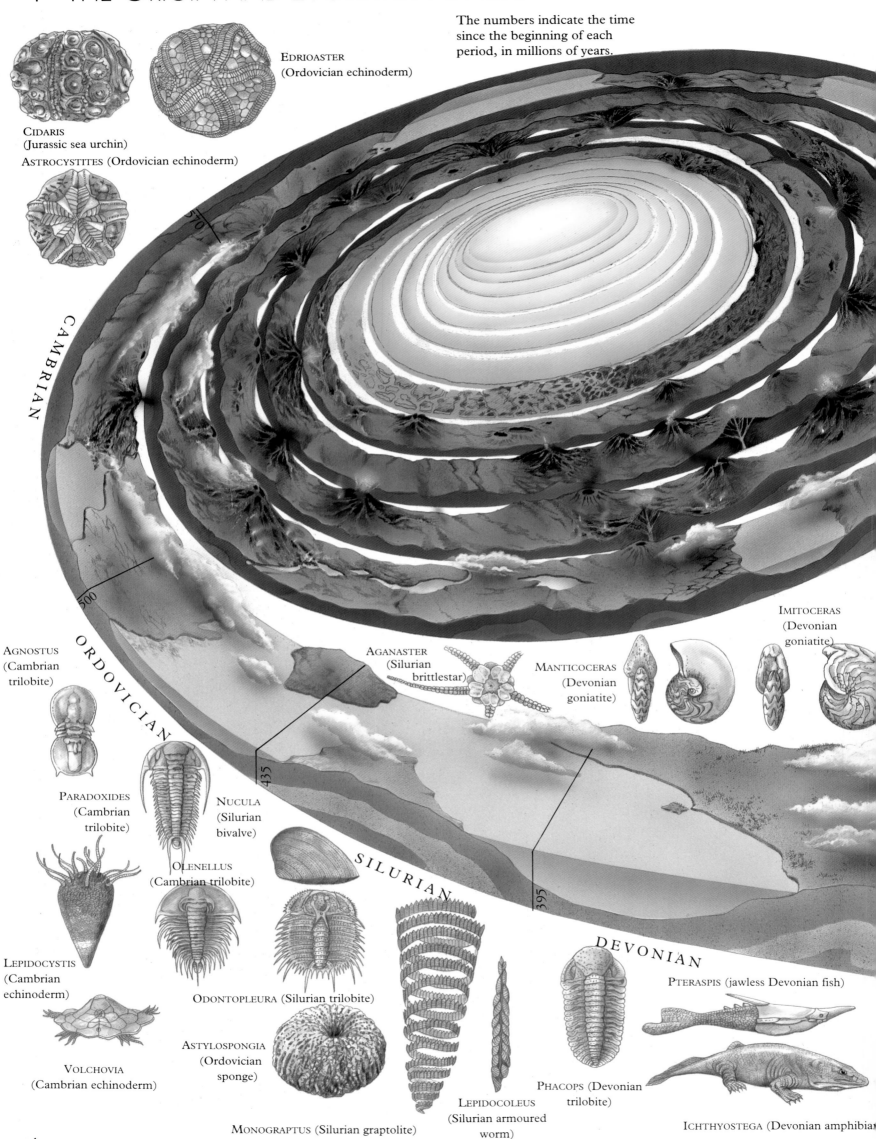

CIDARIS
(Jurassic sea urchin)

EDRIOASTER
(Ordovician echinoderm)

ASTROCYSTITES (Ordovician echinoderm)

CAMBRIAN

570

500

ORDOVICIAN

SILURIAN

DEVONIAN

IMITOCERAS
(Devonian goniatite)

AGANASTER
(Silurian brittlestar)

MANTICOCERAS
(Devonian goniatite)

AGNOSTUS
(Cambrian trilobite)

PARADOXIDES
(Cambrian trilobite)

NUCULA
(Silurian bivalve)

OLENELLUS
(Cambrian trilobite)

435

395

LEPIDOCYSTIS
(Cambrian echinoderm)

ODONTOPLEURA (Silurian trilobite)

PTERASPIS (jawless Devonian fish)

VOLCHOVIA
(Cambrian echinoderm)

ASTYLOSPONGIA
(Ordovician sponge)

PHACOPS (Devonian trilobite)

LEPIDOCOLEUS
(Silurian armoured worm)

MONOGRAPTUS (Silurian graptolite)

ICHTHYOSTEGA (Devonian amphibian)

4

1 In ARCHAEAN times the earth's crust was beginning to solidify, but the atmosphere of ammonia and methane hindered the development of life on the planet for a long time.

2 Life must have started and been incubated in the 'primordial soup' of the Archaean oceans, but the first real signs of life did not appear until PROTEROZOIC times.

3 By CARBONIFEROUS times the atmosphere was rich in oxygen and the life forms that had filled the water began to spread rapidly over the land.

PROTEROZOIC

3.500

4 Proteins and bacteria had appeared by EARLY PROTEROZOIC times.

5 By LATE PROTEROZOIC times protozoans and multicellular algae were living in the water.

ARCHAEAN

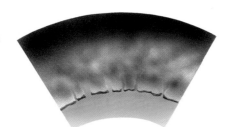

1 ARCHAEAN

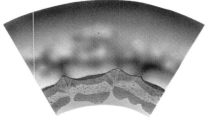

2 PROTEROZOIC

3 CARBONIFEROUS

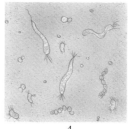

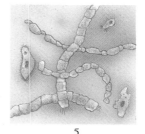

4   5

LEPIDODENDRON

NEUROPTERIS

SOME CARBONIFEROUS PLANTS

CORDAITES

BUETTNERIA (Triassic amphibian)

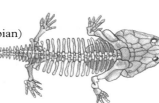

LEBACHIA (an early conifer)

SEYMOURIA (Permian amphibian)

280

UDDENOCERAS
(Devonian goniatite)

CARBONIFEROUS

PERMIAN

EOGYRINUS
(Carboniferous amphibian)

ERYOPS
(large Permian amphibian)

BIRKENIA (Silurian fish)

5

1 THE ORIGIN AND EVOLUTION OF LIFE

Ever since people started to think, they have wondered about the origin of life and how it all started. We have known for over 300 years that living things, including even microscopic bacteria and viruses, can develop only from pre-existing organisms – but how was the very first living thing created? How did life first appear on earth?

Scientists have been able to make amino-acids and proteins – the basic 'building bricks' of which all living things are made – by passing electric currents through mixtures of various gases, but the 'spark' that generated the first life still remains a mystery. It could have been lightning, or simply the sun's strong rays, that caused simple compounds in the air or in the water to react together to produce protein-like materials. However it happened, the new 'proteins' were able to take in extra materials and to grow, and they were able to split up and make more of their own kind. In other words, they were alive.

Geologists believe that the earth came into existence about 4,500 million years ago. It was a ball of very hot gases and dust at first, with a temperature of perhaps 4000°C, but it gradually cooled down and the crust began to solidify. Methane and ammonia gases swirled over the surface, and it must have rained for many thousands of years as the young earth grew cooler. The water formed the oceans, at the edges of which the very first life appeared.

The first life forms
The earliest forms of life probably appeared more than 3,000 million years ago. They were very simple bacteria and algae, and for another 2,000 million years they were the only living things on the planet. They used sunlight as a source of energy for making food, and gave out oxygen in the process, thus paving the way for animal life. The first true cells probably appeared about 1,000 million years ago, and began the spectacular evolution of plants and animals. Simple, single-celled organisms evolved into multicellular ones, and by the beginning of the Cambrian Period (see chart opposite) – about 570 million years ago – they had produced almost all of the major groups of invertebrate animals. In not much more than another 100 million years the invertebrates had given rise to the vertebrates – animals that have backbones. Fish were the first vertebrates, and then came amphibians and reptiles, birds, and mammals. The first human being appeared about 2,500,000 years ago, a descendant of a group of ape-like mammals. The hard bones of many vertebrate animals have been preserved in the rocks as fossils, so we have a good idea of how the animals have evolved over the last 450 million years.

Evolution in the water
The story begins in the freshwater lakes and brackish lagoons of the Ordovician Period. The waters were dominated by huge scorpion-like invertebrates equipped

Most of the rocks around us have been formed from sand and mud that accumulated on the sea bed and gradually hardened into rock, and then, as a result of massive movements of the earth's crust, rose up above sea level. The rocks contain fossils of plants and animals, and the oldest rocks contain the oldest fossils. By studying the different kinds of fossils in each rock layer, scientists have been able to trace the evolution of life. Geologists have also used the different kinds of fossils to divide the earth's history into a number of time zones called eras and periods. The chart opposite shows the main divisions of the earth's history, from its origin some 4,500 million years ago right up to the present day.

with powerful claws, but the first vertebrates were already shuffling over the bottom. They were small fish, most of them covered with bony shields to protect them from the big invertebrates. They had small, round mouths without jaws and they fed by sucking up small bits of food from the sand and mud.

During the Silurian Period, about 430 million years ago, an 'invention' provided a major turning point in the story: the fish developed movable jaws with teeth, which meant that they could tackle a much wider range of food. They quickly lost their bony armour and became fast and elegant swimmers.

During the Devonian Period, some 370 million years ago, the waters were full of all kinds of fish, but already some of them were changing again. Some of them were developing lungs, into which they could gulp air, and their fins were changing into stumpy limbs. These fish were able to haul themselves out of the water and into the surrounding humid swamps, where they found plenty of insects and other small animals to eat among the ferns and horsetails. These pioneering fish gave rise to the first amphibians, which evolved into a wide range of forms during the Carboniferous Period.

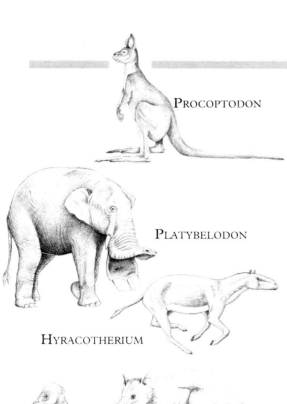

PROCOPTODON

PLATYBELODON

HYRACOTHERIUM

ALPHADON

PACHYCEPHALOSAURUS

ARCHAEOPTERYX

THRINAXODON

DIMETRODON

EUSTHENOPTERON

CEPHALASPIS

PTERASPIS

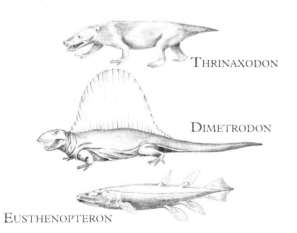

ARANDASPIS

TRILOBITE

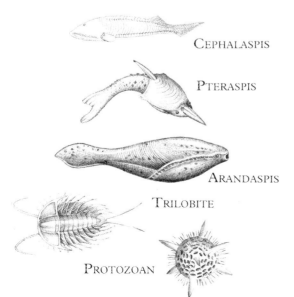

PROTOZOAN

Era	Period	Major Events	Epoch	Years ago, in Millions of Years
NEOZOIC	HOLOCENE	Middle and New Stone Ages (Post-glacial). The beginning of history (about 6,000 years ago)		10,000 years ago
NEOZOIC	PLEISTOCENE	Appearance and extinction of Neanderthal Man (Middle Old Stone Age). Appearance of modern Man (Upper Old Stone Age). Würm glaciation	UPPER	150,000 years ago
NEOZOIC	PLEISTOCENE	Appearance of *Homo sapiens* at the end of the epoch. Mindel & Riss glaciations. Extinction of australopithecines	MIDDLE	700,000 years ago
NEOZOIC	PLEISTOCENE	Appearance of *Homo erectus* (Lower Old Stone Age). Donau & Gunz glaciations	LOWER	2
CENOZOIC	UPPER TERTIARY (NEOGENE)	Appearance of man (*Homo habilis* about 2.5 million years ago?). Appearance of australopithecines	PLIOCENE	5
CENOZOIC	UPPER TERTIARY (NEOGENE)	Appearance of dryopithecine apes. The linking of Africa and Europe	MIOCENE	22
CENOZOIC	LOWER TERTIARY (PALAEOGENE)	The monkeys give rise to the first apes	OLIGOCENE	40
CENOZOIC	LOWER TERTIARY (PALAEOGENE)	Appearance of lemurs and the first monkeys	EOCENE	55
CENOZOIC	LOWER TERTIARY (PALAEOGENE)	Appearance of the earliest prosimians	PALAEOCENE	65
MESOZOIC	CRETACEOUS	Appearance of the first primates. Extinction of the dinosaurs	UPPER	100
MESOZOIC	CRETACEOUS	Rapid evolution of birds. The first flowering plants	LOWER	140
MESOZOIC	JURASSIC	A huge variety of dinosaurs	UPPER	160
MESOZOIC	JURASSIC	The first birds	MIDDLE	176
MESOZOIC	JURASSIC	The first flying reptiles (pterosaurs)	LOWER	195
MESOZOIC	TRIASSIC	Major development of the dinosaurs	UPPER	215
MESOZOIC	TRIASSIC	Appearance of the first mammals	MIDDLE	225
MESOZOIC	TRIASSIC	Appearance of the dinosaurs. The break-up of Gondwanaland	LOWER	245
PALAEOZOIC	PERMIAN	Reptiles covered the land	UPPER	260
PALAEOZOIC	PERMIAN	A big increase in coniferous plants	LOWER	280
PALAEOZOIC	CARBONIFEROUS	The first reptiles. The coal forests covered large areas of land	UPPER	330
PALAEOZOIC	CARBONIFEROUS	The first seed-bearing plants	LOWER	345
PALAEOZOIC	DEVONIAN	The first amphibians	UPPER	360
PALAEOZOIC	DEVONIAN	Insects and other invertebrates appeared on dry land	MIDDLE	370
PALAEOZOIC	DEVONIAN	The first ferns. Goniatites appeared in the seas	LOWER	395
PALAEOZOIC	SILURIAN	Plants first invaded the land	UPPER	420
PALAEOZOIC	SILURIAN	The first jawed fishes and coral reefs appeared	LOWER	435
PALAEOZOIC	ORDOVICIAN	The first sea urchins	UPPER	450
PALAEOZOIC	ORDOVICIAN	The first backboned animals (armoured fishes). Trilobites and graptolites were abundant	LOWER	500
PALAEOZOIC	CAMBRIAN	Appearance of oceanic plankton. Rapid spread of trilobites and marine algae	UPPER	520
PALAEOZOIC	CAMBRIAN	All major invertebrate groups appeared in the oceans	LOWER	570
PRE-CAMBRIAN	PROTEROZOIC	The first signs of life, beginning with bacteria and simple algae		2600
PRE-CAMBRIAN	ARCHAEAN	Formation of the earth and solidification of the crust		4500

2 FROM REPTILES TO MAMMALS

The earth has been slowly changing ever since its formation some 4,500 million years ago. The rocky plates forming its crust have moved across the surface, sometimes colliding with each other and throwing up mountains and sometimes slipping under each other to create the ocean depths.

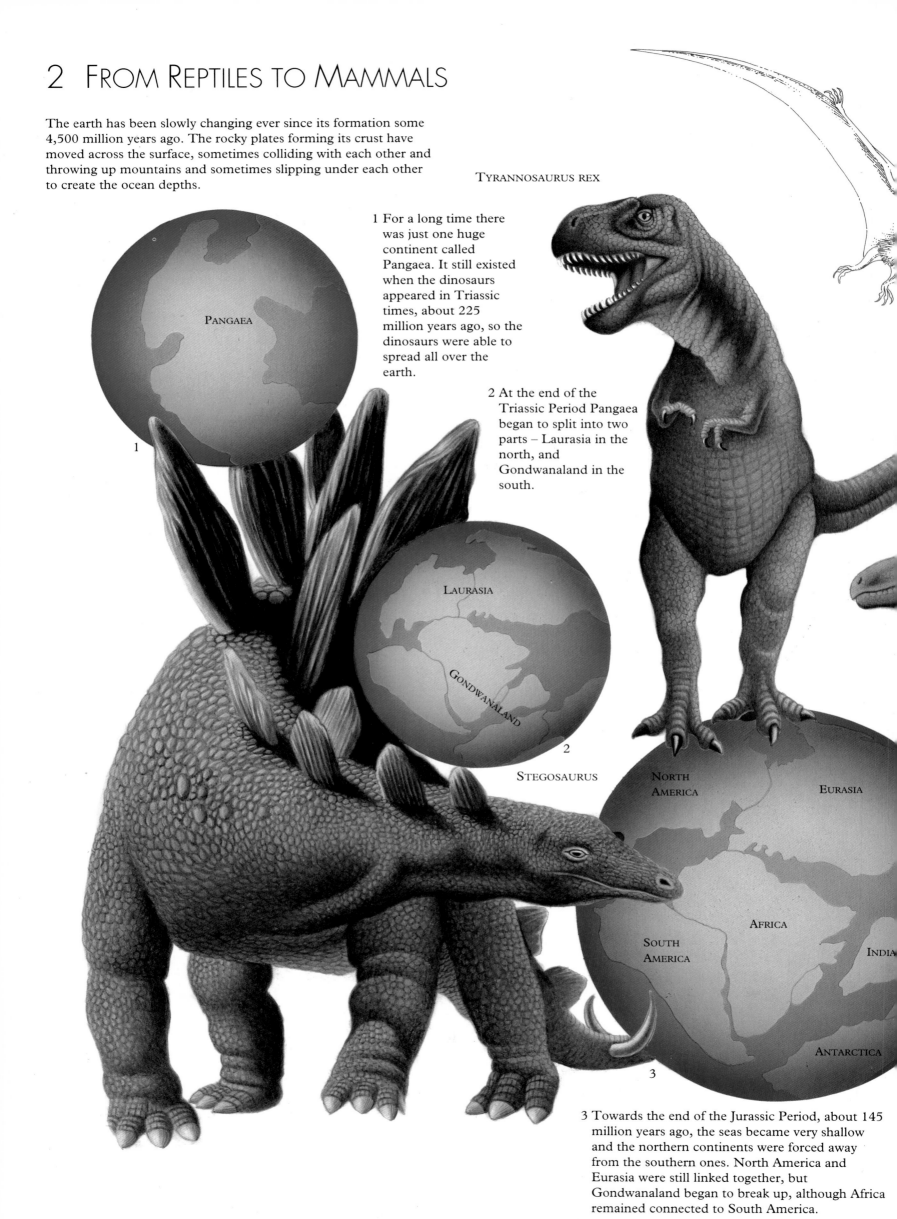

TYRANNOSAURUS REX

1 For a long time there was just one huge continent called Pangaea. It still existed when the dinosaurs appeared in Triassic times, about 225 million years ago, so the dinosaurs were able to spread all over the earth.

2 At the end of the Triassic Period Pangaea began to split into two parts – Laurasia in the north, and Gondwanaland in the south.

PANGAEA

1

LAURASIA

GONDWANALAND

2

STEGOSAURUS

NORTH AMERICA

EURASIA

AFRICA

SOUTH AMERICA

INDIA

ANTARCTICA

3

3 Towards the end of the Jurassic Period, about 145 million years ago, the seas became very shallow and the northern continents were forced away from the southern ones. North America and Eurasia were still linked together, but Gondwanaland began to break up, although Africa remained connected to South America.

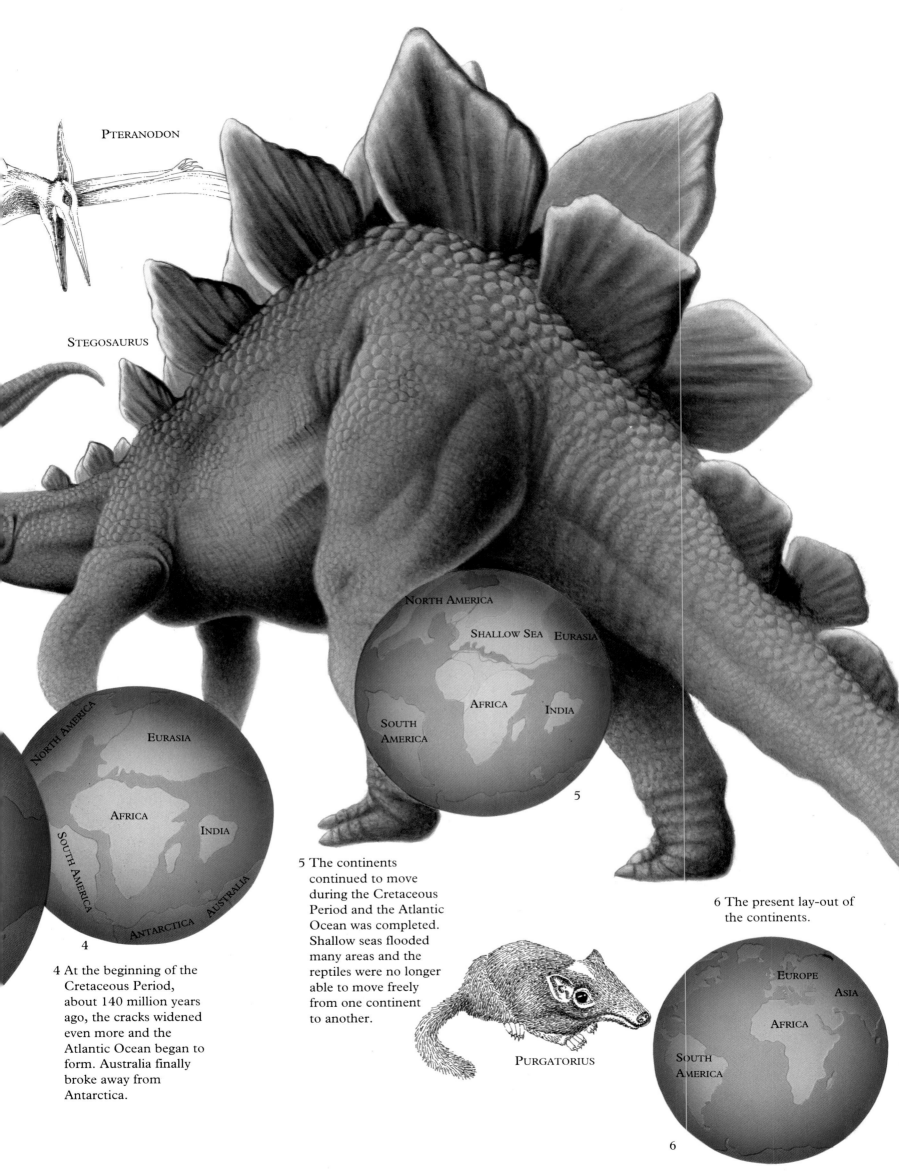

PTERANODON

STEGOSAURUS

NORTH AMERICA

SHALLOW SEA   EURASIA

AFRICA   INDIA

SOUTH
AMERICA

5

NORTH AMERICA

EURASIA

AFRICA   INDIA

SOUTH AMERICA

ANTARCTICA   AUSTRALIA

4

4 At the beginning of the
Cretaceous Period,
about 140 million years
ago, the cracks widened
even more and the
Atlantic Ocean began to
form. Australia finally
broke away from
Antarctica.

5 The continents
continued to move
during the Cretaceous
Period and the Atlantic
Ocean was completed.
Shallow seas flooded
many areas and the
reptiles were no longer
able to move freely
from one continent
to another.

6 The present lay-out of
the continents.

PURGATORIUS

EUROPE

ASIA

AFRICA

SOUTH
AMERICA

6

2 FROM REPTILES TO MAMMALS

The warm, humid conditions that existed in many parts of the world during the greater part of the Carboniferous Period were ideal for the early amphibians. Just like most of today's amphibians, they were confined to damp places and they had to return to the water to breed. But the climate began to change towards the end of the Carboniferous, and much drier conditions spread over a large area of the land. The amphibians in general could not cope with the changes, but one group was already prepared, or adapted, to meet the challenge. Its members had developed tough, waterproof skins and, even more important, they had started to lay eggs with tough, waterproof shells. These new animals were the first reptiles.

Spectacular reptiles

Freed from the need to stay in wet places, reptiles were able to push into territory forbidden to their amphibian ancestors. During the Permian Period reptiles spread all over the earth which, at that time, was made up of one single big land mass called Pangaea. The climate was warm, and remained so for some 180 million years. It was ideal for the reptiles, whose body temperatures depended on those of their surroundings. During the Mesozoic Era the reptiles evolved in numerous directions to produce thousands of strange and often spectacular forms. Most of them lived on the land, but some went into the seas and some even took up flying. The dinosaurs appeared during the Triassic Period, about 240 million years ago, and ruled the world for over 100 million years until they mysteriously disappeared during the Cretaceous Period. They included the largest terrestrial animals that have ever lived on the earth. But not all dinosaurs were big: some were no larger than chickens. There were also some very curious horned and armoured dinosaurs.

One important line of reptile evolution produced a group called therapsids. These lived during Permian and Triassic times, and from their fossilized teeth we know that they included both herbivorous and carnivorous forms. By dinosaur standards, they were unremarkable creatures, but somewhere among the therapsids were the forerunners of the mammals, the group to which we ourselves belong.

The first mammals

The first mammals appeared during the Triassic Period, about 220 million years ago, but they found themselves in competition with the dinosaurs and they were able to survive only by becoming nocturnal. Their eyes improved, and the senses of smell and hearing became particularly acute, enabling the animals to find their way about in the dark. The mammals did not need the sun's warmth because they were able to maintain their bodies at a constant temperature, but this took a lot of energy and they needed a good supply of easily digested food.

From the middle of the Permian Period, the earth's climate remained warm and fairly constant for about 180 million years, and encouraged the rapid evolution of the reptiles. The earth's continents were joined together in one large mass called Pangaea until the end of the Triassic Period, so the early reptiles were able to spread into all regions.

The fossil record shows that even during the Jurassic and Cretaceous Periods, after the break-up of Pangaea, certain species of large reptiles were present on separate continents. It is thought that the existence of temporary land-bridges made this possible.

They probably ate a lot of insects and possibly the eggs of dinosaurs and other reptiles. They were furry creatures and their fur helped them to keep warm.

The first mammals laid eggs, but by late Cretaceous times they had given rise to pouched mammals, or marsupials, that carry their babies in pouches. The marsupials had spread nearly all over the earth by the end of the Cretaceous Period, but were then gradually replaced in most areas by placental mammals. Almost all of today's mammals are placentals – so-called because at first their babies develop inside their mother's body and feed through an organ called the placenta. Australia still has lots of marsupials because it had separated from the rest of the continents by the time that the placental mammals started to evolve, so they could not reach it.

The mammals take over

When the dinosaurs died out at the end of the Cretaceous Period the mammals branched out and began to fill the habitats left by the great reptiles. During the early part of the Tertiary Period a wide range of bizarre 'experimental' mammals appeared, but many of them quickly died out. By Upper Tertiary times, about 20 million years ago, mammals included whales, hoofed mammals, rodents, primates, and other animals very much like those we see around us today. In a relatively short space of time the primates gave rise to a branch leading to the first humans.

The early primates flourished in the warm forests of Europe, Africa and North America. The oldest known primate was *Purgatorius*, whose fossil remains were discovered in 1965 in the Rocky Mountains of Montana in the United States. The place had been called Purgatory Hill, because the work was hard and the fossils were few. The fossil remains, consisting of some teeth and jaw bones, show that *Purgatorius* was no bigger than a mole. It had 44 teeth and probably fed on fruit and insects in the trees. It lived about 70 million years ago.

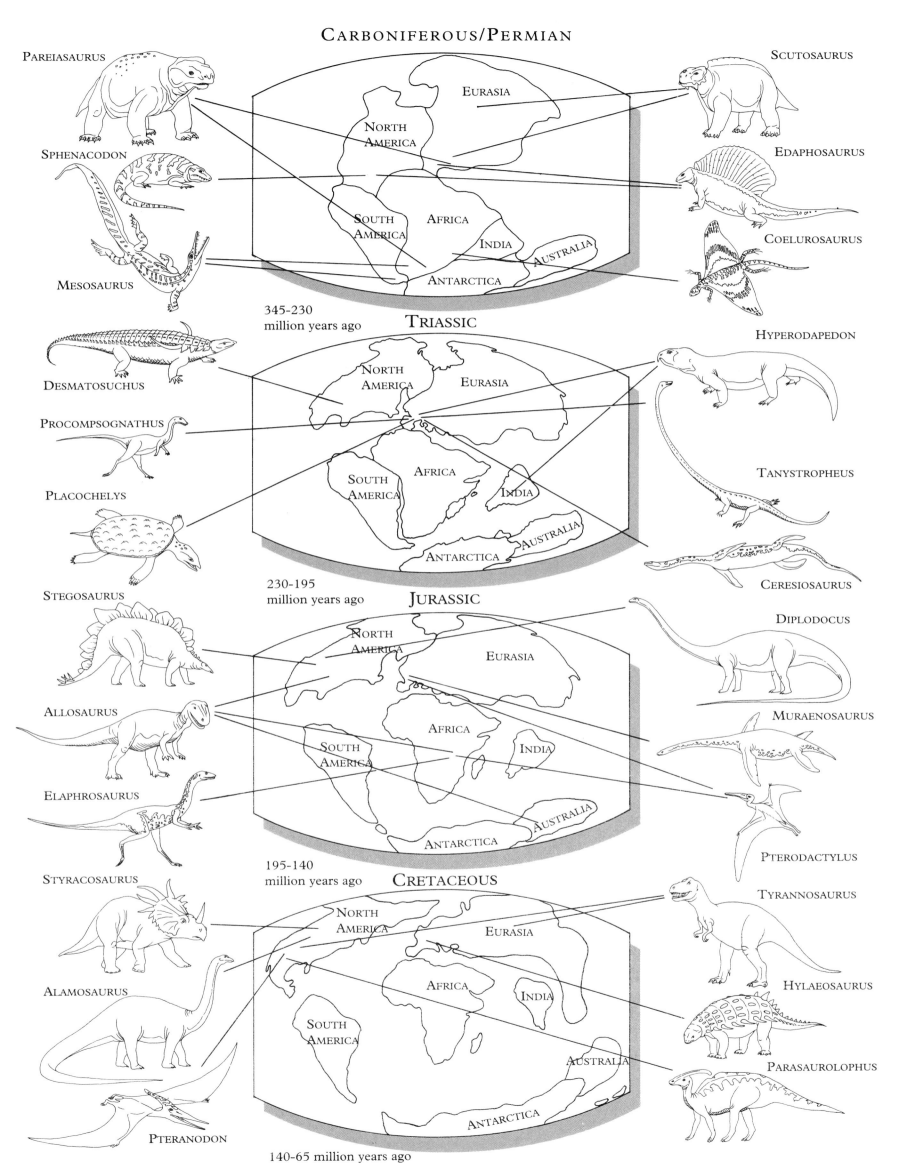

CARBONIFEROUS/PERMIAN

PAREIASAURUS

SPHENACODON

MESOSAURUS

EURASIA

NORTH AMERICA

SOUTH AMERICA

AFRICA

INDIA

AUSTRALIA

ANTARCTICA

345-230 million years ago

SCUTOSAURUS

EDAPHOSAURUS

COELUROSAURUS

TRIASSIC

DESMATOSUCHUS

PROCOMPSOGNATHUS

PLACOCHELYS

NORTH AMERICA

EURASIA

SOUTH AMERICA

AFRICA

INDIA

AUSTRALIA

ANTARCTICA

230-195 million years ago

HYPERODAPEDON

TANYSTROPHEUS

CERESIOSAURUS

JURASSIC

STEGOSAURUS

ALLOSAURUS

ELAPHROSAURUS

NORTH AMERICA

EURASIA

AFRICA

SOUTH AMERICA

INDIA

AUSTRALIA

ANTARCTICA

195-140 million years ago

DIPLODOCUS

MURAENOSAURUS

PTERODACTYLUS

CRETACEOUS

STYRACOSAURUS

ALAMOSAURUS

PTERANODON

NORTH AMERICA

EURASIA

AFRICA

INDIA

SOUTH AMERICA

AUSTRALIA

ANTARCTICA

140-65 million years ago

TYRANNOSAURUS

HYLAEOSAURUS

PARASAUROLOPHUS

11

3 FROM EARLY PRIMATES TO HOMINIDS

The distribution of *Proconsul africanus* more than 17 million years ago, when Africa and Eurasia were still separated.

The distribution of *Proconsul* and related dryopithecines less than 17 million years ago, when Eurasia and Africa had linked up.

PROCONSUL

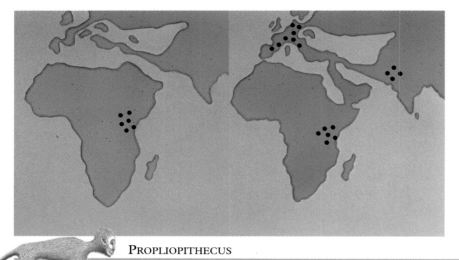

PROPLIOPITHECUS

OLIGOPITHECUS

AEGYPTOPITHECUS

Distribution of *Aegyptopithecus*

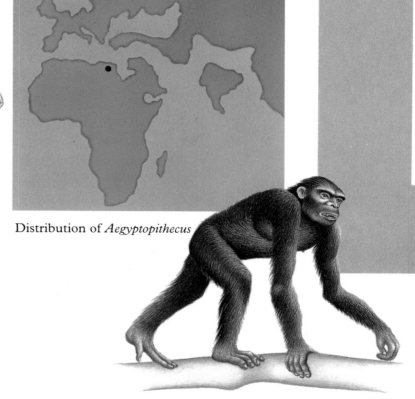

DRYOPITHECUS

Oligopithecus, about 30cm long, was the earliest catarrhine monkey with teeth similar to our own. It lived in Egypt about 35 million years ago.

Propliopithecus, another early catarrhine primate, lived in Egypt some 30 million years ago. It was the size of a small gibbon and walked on four legs on the ground and in the trees.

Aegyptopithecus also lived in Egypt about 30 million years ago. It had a long tail and powerful jaw muscles.

The distribution of sites where the remains of dryopithecines and ramapithecines have been discovered. The dryopithecine finds are the oldest and refer to *Proconsul africanus*, while the ramapithecine remains could have been derived from *Kenyapithecus* and the Eurasian *Dryopithecus*.

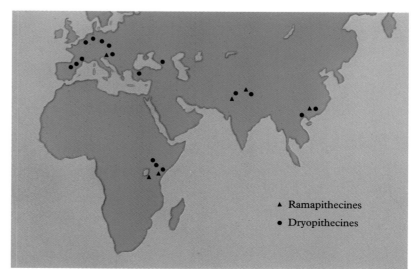

▲ Ramapithecines
● Dryopithecines

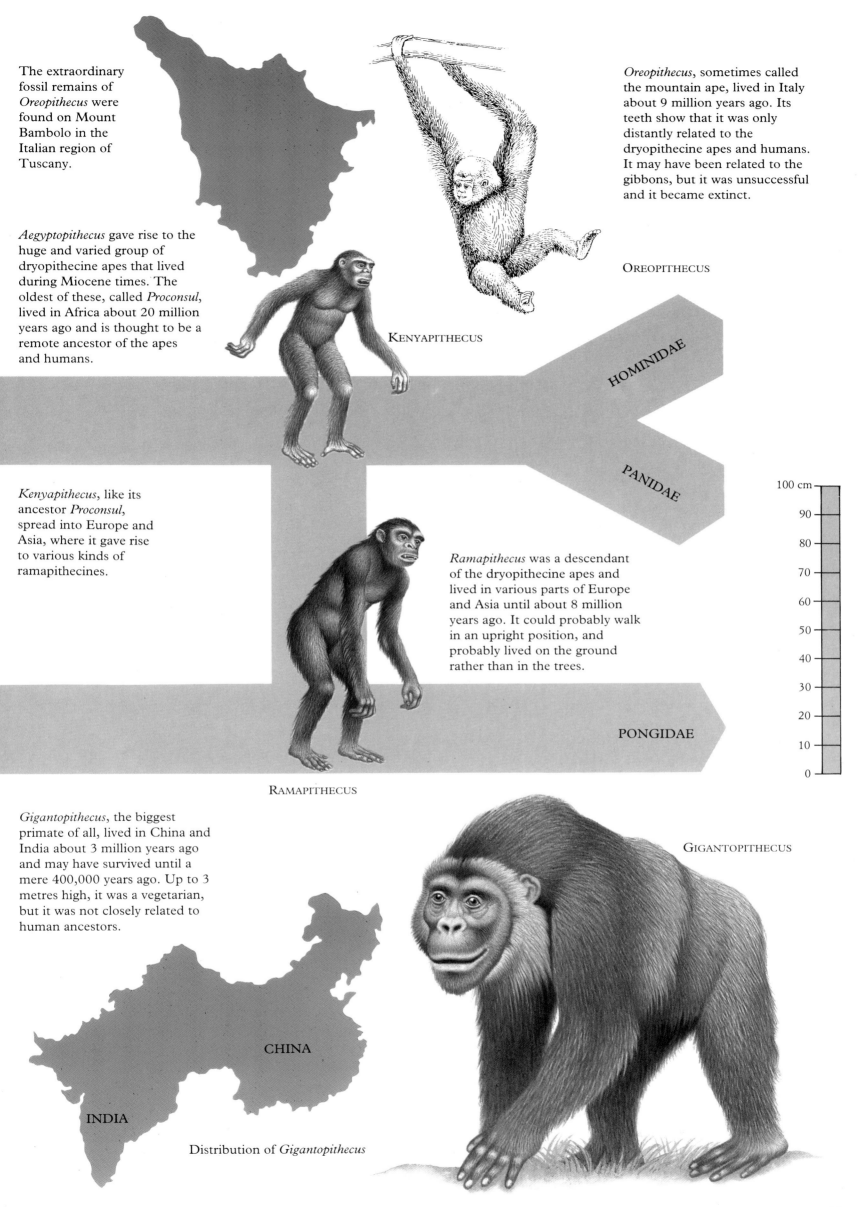

The extraordinary fossil remains of *Oreopithecus* were found on Mount Bambolo in the Italian region of Tuscany.

Aegyptopithecus gave rise to the huge and varied group of dryopithecine apes that lived during Miocene times. The oldest of these, called *Proconsul*, lived in Africa about 20 million years ago and is thought to be a remote ancestor of the apes and humans.

Kenyapithecus, like its ancestor *Proconsul*, spread into Europe and Asia, where it gave rise to various kinds of ramapithecines.

Oreopithecus, sometimes called the mountain ape, lived in Italy about 9 million years ago. Its teeth show that it was only distantly related to the dryopithecine apes and humans. It may have been related to the gibbons, but it was unsuccessful and it became extinct.

OREOPITHECUS

KENYAPITHECUS

HOMINIDAE

PANIDAE

Ramapithecus was a descendant of the dryopithecine apes and lived in various parts of Europe and Asia until about 8 million years ago. It could probably walk in an upright position, and probably lived on the ground rather than in the trees.

PONGIDAE

RAMAPITHECUS

100 cm
90
80
70
60
50
40
30
20
10
0

Gigantopithecus, the biggest primate of all, lived in China and India about 3 million years ago and may have survived until a mere 400,000 years ago. Up to 3 metres high, it was a vegetarian, but it was not closely related to human ancestors.

GIGANTOPITHECUS

CHINA

INDIA

Distribution of *Gigantopithecus*

13

3 FROM EARLY PRIMATES TO HOMINIDS

Although the primates now include the most intelligent and advanced of all animals, they actually appeared quite early in the evolution of mammals. *Purgatorius* was alive at the end of the Cretaceous Period, and by Palaeocene times, about 60 million years ago, the earth was populated by a wide range of monkey-ancestors called prosimians. *Plesiadapis*, whose remains have been discovered in Europe and North America, was the size of a large cat and had already become quite specialized for life in the trees. It was nocturnal and probably fed on insects.

Most of the other early prosimians were less specialized, but during Eocene times, when the earth was covered with huge areas of warm forest, they began to evolve rapidly. They eventually gave rise to the tree shrews and tarsiers of South-east Asia, the lemurs of Madagascar, and the African bushbabies, while another major branch led to monkeys. The monkey branch is also known as the anthropoid branch, a name that means 'manlike'.

Old World and New World monkeys

While monkeys were evolving from their prosimian ancestors during Eocene times, North America split away from Eurasia and Africa. The monkeys in the two regions developed independently, so we now have two rather different groups of monkeys – American or New World monkeys, known as platyrrhines, and Old World monkeys, or catarrhines. During Oligocene times, perhaps about 35 million years ago, a group of Old World monkeys gave rise to the first apes, and a few million years later the apes gave rise to the first hominids – the first members of the human family.

Tree dwellers

The reason for the primates' success was, surprisingly, a lack of specialization, especially in their limbs. They could not fly or burrow and they could not swim or run very well either. But they could climb well and they lived mainly in the trees, out of the way of most predators. Their mobile hands and feet, each with five fingers or toes, were very valuable for clinging to the branches and picking fruit. The primates also evolved excellent eyesight, with forward-looking eyes, and good brains to control their tree-top movements.

The oldest undoubted remains of the catarrhines come from the Oligocene rocks of the Fayum Basin in Egypt. Some of these belong to a primitive group called the parapithecines, but the rest belong to two more advanced groups of monkeys and apes – the cercopithecines and the propliopithecines. *Oligopithecus* was the first known monkey to have teeth like our own. *Aegyptopithecus* was a forest-dwelling ape and may have been an ancestor of the dryopithecine apes, such as *Proconsul africanus*. The latter lived in East Africa and was the size of a small gorilla. It is thought that *Proconsul*

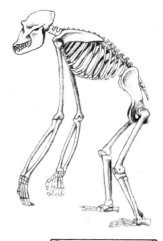

The skeleton of an orang-utan (left) and a chimpanzee. The latter spent less time in the trees and so its skeleton developed a more upright position.

The New World monkeys have flat noses, with nostrils opening to the sides. Some have prehensile tails that can grasp.

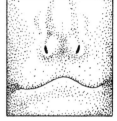

Gibbons swing through the trees with their arms. This kind of movement is called brachiation.

Old World monkeys have more obvious noses, with downward-pointing nostrils. None of them has a prehensile tail.

and its allies gave rise, through the later dryopithecine and ramapithecine apes, to the first hominids.

Down from the trees

During Miocene times, about 17 million years ago, Africa linked up with Eurasia. The climate became cooler and drier, and many previously forested areas gradually turned into grasslands. This was probably when the apes started to come down from the trees and live on the ground. The monkeys and apes spread from Africa into Eurasia and continued their evolution. The cercopithecines gave rise to *Mesopithecus* and *Dolichopithecus* and to the various kinds of macaque monkeys that live in Asia today.

The pliopithecines soon diverged from the other apes and gave rise to the gibbons that now live in Asia. At the same time the dryopithecines continued to evolve and they gave rise to a wide range of apes, including the colossal *Gigantopithecus* and the ancestors of human beings and today's great apes.

FAMILY TREE OF THE PRIMATES

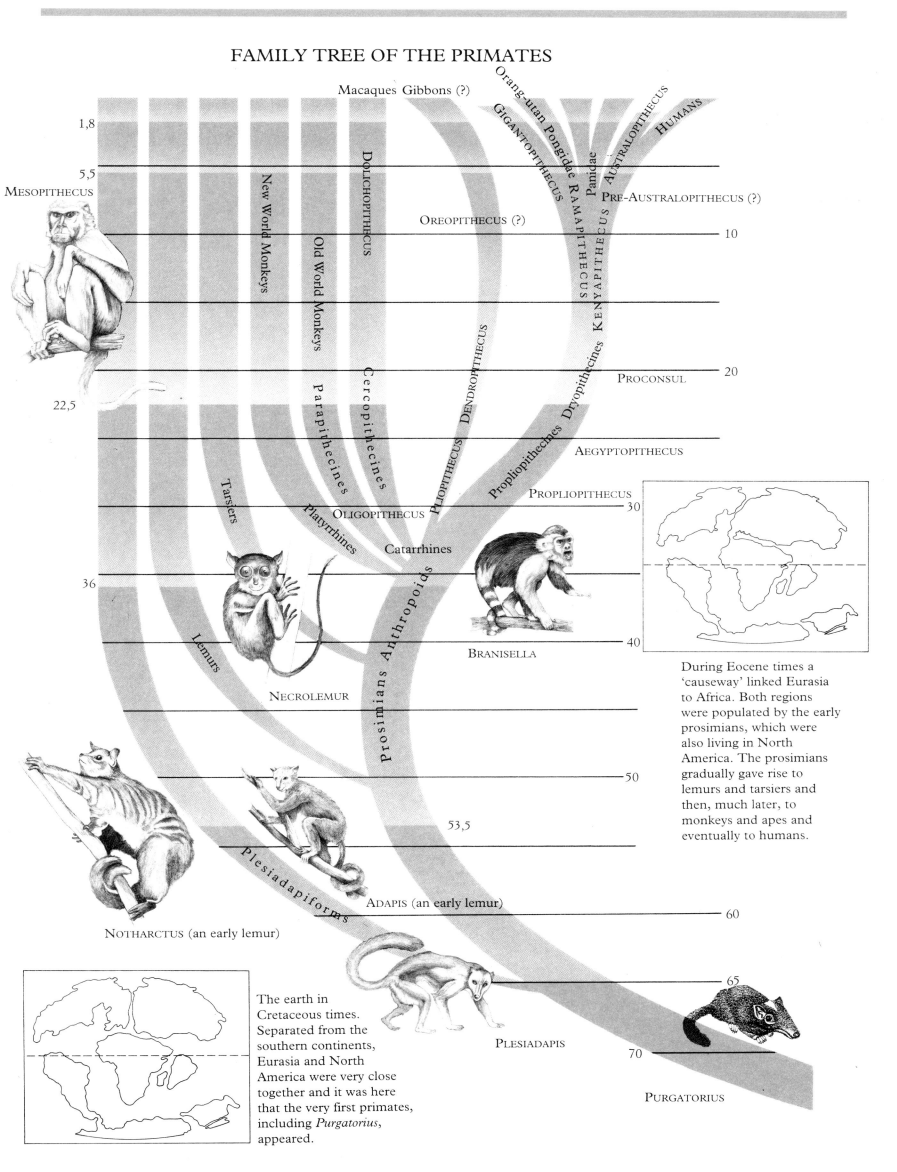

Macaques Gibbons (?)

Orang-utan Pongidae Panidae HUMANS

GIGANTOPITHECUS RAMAPITHECUS AUSTRALOPITHECUS

1,8

5,5

MESOPITHECUS

DOLICHOPITHECUS

New World Monkeys

Old World Monkeys

OREOPITHECUS (?)

PRE-AUSTRALOPITHECUS (?)

KENYAPITHECUS

10

22,5

Parapithecines

Cercopithecines

DENDROPITHECUS

Dryopithecines

PROCONSUL

20

PLIOPITHECUS

Propliopithecines

AEGYPTOPITHECUS

Tarsiers

Platyrrhines

OLIGOPITHECUS

PROPLIOPITHECUS

30

Catarrhines

Anthropoids

Prosimians

BRANISELLA

36

Lemurs

NECROLEMUR

40

During Eocene times a 'causeway' linked Eurasia to Africa. Both regions were populated by the early prosimians, which were also living in North America. The prosimians gradually gave rise to lemurs and tarsiers and then, much later, to monkeys and apes and eventually to humans.

50

53,5

Plesiadapiforms

ADAPIS (an early lemur)

60

NOTHARCTUS (an early lemur)

65

The earth in Cretaceous times. Separated from the southern continents, Eurasia and North America were very close together and it was here that the very first primates, including *Purgatorius*, appeared.

PLESIADAPIS

70

PURGATORIUS

15

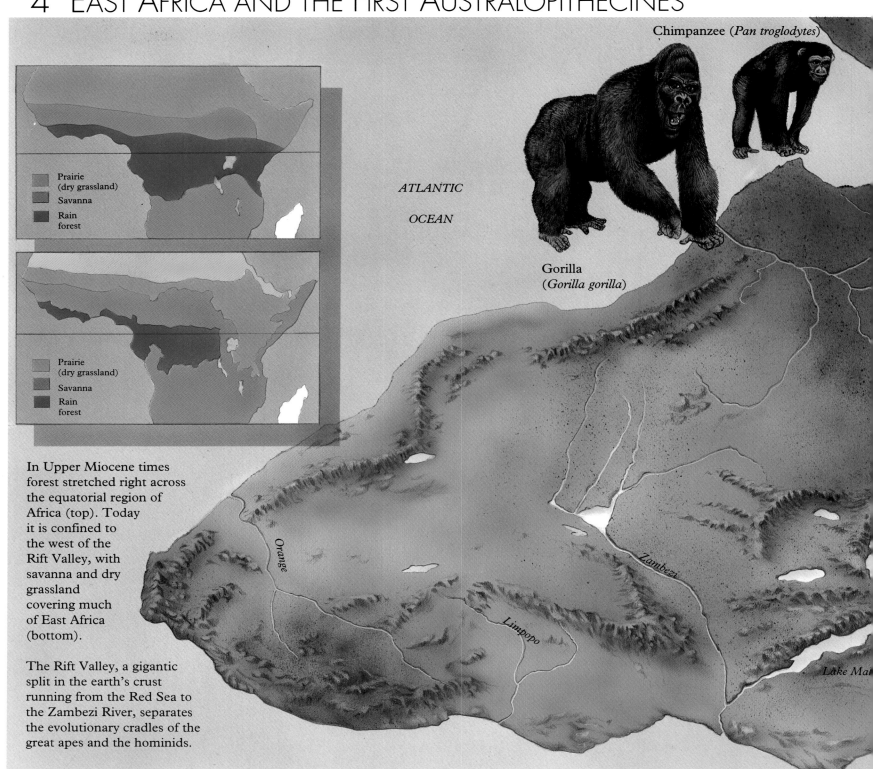

Chimpanzee (*Pan troglodytes*)

Gorilla
(*Gorilla gorilla*)

ATLANTIC

OCEAN

Prairie
(dry grassland)
Savanna
Rain
forest

Prairie
(dry grassland)
Savanna
Rain
forest

Orange

Zambezi

Limpopo

Lake Ma

In Upper Miocene times
forest stretched right across
the equatorial region of
Africa (top). Today
it is confined to
the west of the
Rift Valley, with
savanna and dry
grassland
covering much
of East Africa
(bottom).

The Rift Valley, a gigantic
split in the earth's crust
running from the Red Sea to
the Zambezi River, separates
the evolutionary cradles of the
great apes and the hominids.

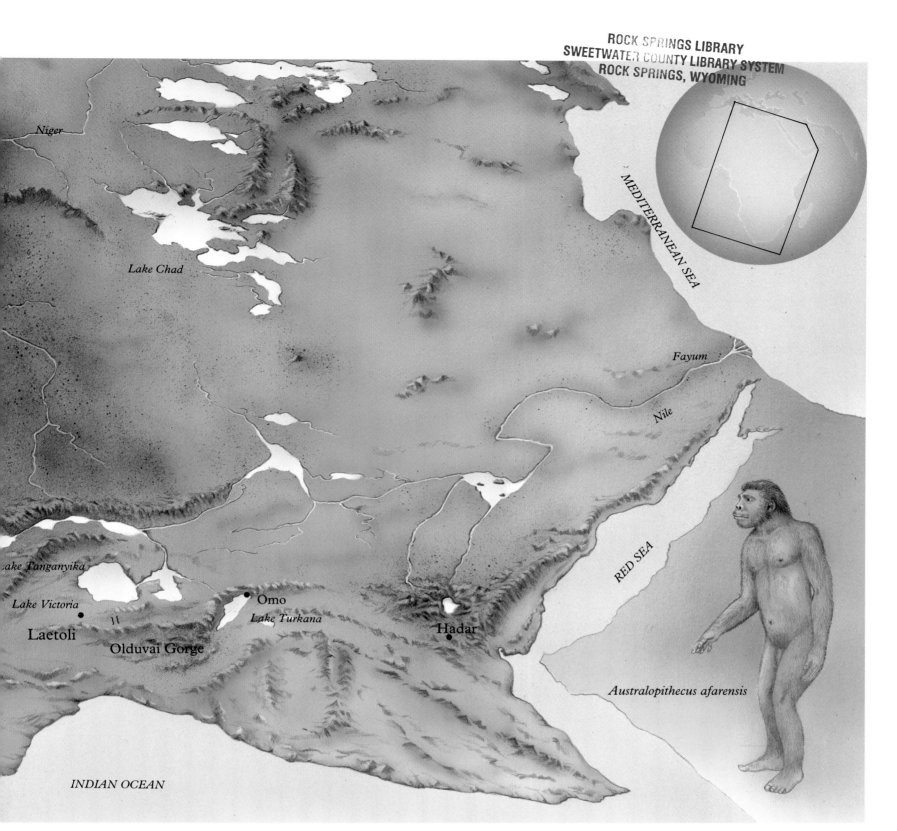

Niger

Lake Chad

MEDITERRANEAN SEA

Fayum

Nile

Lake Tanganyika

Lake Victoria

Omo

Lake Turkana

Laetoli

Olduvai Gorge

Hadar

RED SEA

Australopithecus afarensis

INDIAN OCEAN

4 EAST AFRICA AND THE FIRST AUSTRALOPITHECINES

It is obvious that there is a connection between humans and the great apes and that the two groups had a common ancestor back in the Tertiary Period. But how and when did the two groups divide and start to develop their own characteristics? One of the major differences between the hominids – the human family – and the great apes lies in the skeleton. The apes continued to swing through the trees on their long arms, and to walk in a crouched position, but the early hominids lived on the ground and walked in a more upright position. The adoption of an upright posture was very important and came to be considered the 'one-jump-ahead' that eventually allowed the human species to outstrip all other animals. By walking only on their back legs, hominids were able to use their hands for other purposes and this gave them a big advantage.

The transformation did not happen suddenly, and we must not think that the long-armed apes, tired of living in the trees, came down to the ground and started to walk on their back legs. In fact, the change could not have happened in the forest: it must have taken place in an open situation, at the edge of the forest or out on the savanna, where upright creatures had an advantage. The change took place very slowly, and probably started several million years before the hominids left their footprints in the volcanic ash of Laetoli in Tanzania about 3.6 million years ago.

Change in the environment

Until Upper Miocene times, tropical forest stretched right across Africa from the Atlantic to the Indian Ocean. But then colossal movements of the earth's crust caused a huge crack to slice through Africa. The crack is called the Rift Valley and it runs from the Red Sea to the Zambezi River. The high cliffs associated with the rift altered the rainfall pattern and the eastern

Equator

::: Distribution of gorillas and chimpanzees

▨ Distribution of ancient hominids

▬ Rift Valley

side became much drier. To the west of the rift the climate remained rainy and the land stayed forested. The apes there continued to live as they had done for millions of years. But on the eastern side of the rift the forests shrank and the countryside became much more open – just right for the upright hominids. This was the world of the australopithecines.

The name australopithecine means 'southern ape', but these creatures were more than apes. Their brains and teeth were ape-like, but they undoubtedly walked upright and they were clearly hominids – early humans. They appeared in East Africa about 5 million years ago, and perhaps even earlier, and flourished there until less than a

The scene (pictured in colour on pages 16/17) shows the 'first family' of *Australopithecus afarensis*, who lived at Hadar over 3 million years ago. To defend themselves against predators, the groups spent the nights in the trees scattered over the savanna on which they lived.

To construct refuges in the trees, the australopithecines had to work together, especially when there were babies to be cared for. The youngsters were cared for mainly by their mothers, but the fathers helped as well.

The australopithecines spent

the whole day searching for food. They were not yet hunters and, although they probably took meat from animals killed by predators, they fed almost entirely on fruit and other plant food.

The female in the foreground is picking fruit from the trees,

while further away two females dig tubers from the dry ground. On the right, another individual drinks from a water hole in the same manner as the animals.

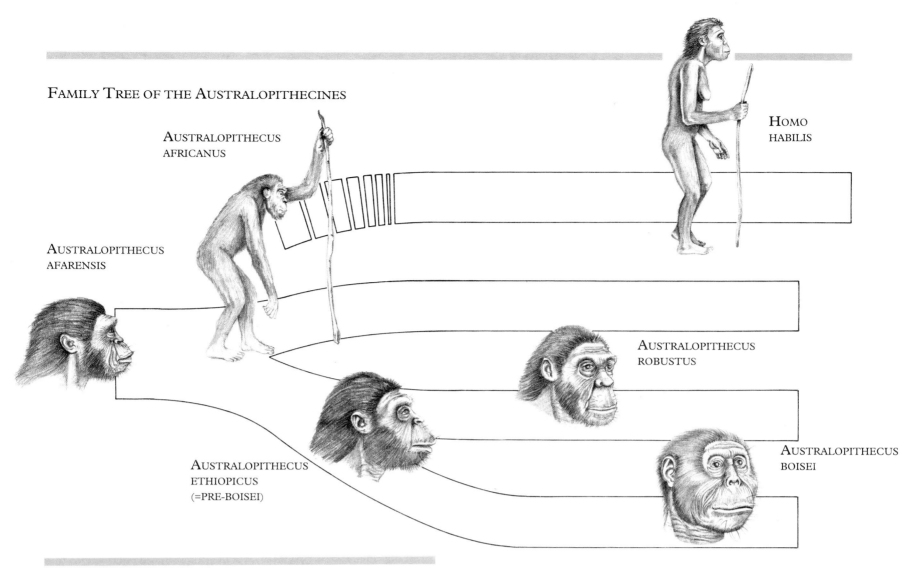

AUSTRALOPITHECUS
AFRICANUS

HOMO
HABILIS

AUSTRALOPITHECUS
AFARENSIS

AUSTRALOPITHECUS
ROBUSTUS

AUSTRALOPITHECUS
ETHIOPICUS
(=PRE-BOISEI)

AUSTRALOPITHECUS
BOISEI

million years ago. They can be justly called our ancestors, but they are also our cousins because they lived side by side with true humans for about a million years.

Lucy – the first lady

In 1974, in the Hadar Basin about 60km (37 miles) from Addis Ababa in Ethiopia, an international expedition found the remains of a hominid over 3 million years old. There were 52 bones, all from the same individual, and because it was clearly a female the finders called it Lucy. Officially, the creature was named *Australopithecus afarensis*, because it had been discovered at Afar. The skeleton showed that 'Lucy' walked in an upright position and was not much more than a metre (3ft 3in) tall. She had long arms, a small head with a prominent jaw, large front teeth, and square cheek teeth for efficient chewing. She probably weighed about 30kg (66lb).

The first family

Other examples of *Australopithecus afarensis* have since been found, and it has been possible to discover something of their daily lives. Another important find at Hadar consisted of the remains of a dozen individuals of both sexes and various ages, who had all died together. This so-called 'first family' showed that the australopithecines lived in groups. They spent the daytime looking for food and their teeth show that they were vegetarians. Picking fruit and seeds to be eaten on the spot presented no problems, but digging roots and tubers from the sun-baked earth was more difficult. The australopithecines shared the water holes with grazing animals that were quite unafraid of them. At sunset, these early ancestors of ours probably climbed into the trees to keep out of the way of prowling lions and other hunting animals.

Australopithecus afarensis is now widely regarded as the most generalized of the australopithecine species, and the most probable candidate for the role of 'first ancestor' of the human line – the ancestor from which all human forms have descended. There is no doubt, however, that *afarensis* also gave rise to several 'experimental' lines of australopithecines that evolved alongside the human line before dying out.

On 30 November 1974, near the dried-up River Hadar in Ethiopia, an international expedition led by Don Johanson and Yves Coppens discovered part of a female skeleton that was older and more complete than any previously known upright human ancestor. The skeleton was given the name Lucy, from the title of the Beatles' song *Lucy in the Sky with Diamonds* that the expedition members sang in their camp.

5 AUSTRALOPITHECUS AND HOMO HABILIS

The big carnivores, especially the leopard, would often take their prey into a tree to protect it from jackals and hyenas. The hominids also had to defend themselves and their food against hunting animals.

Australopithecines and *Homo habilis* lived together on the vast grasslands of East and South Africa between three million and one million years ago. The map below shows the main sites at which their fossils have been found. The figures in the captions indicate the approximate ages of the fossils in millions of years.

TAUNG
Australopithecus africanus
(young) (2.0)

SWARTKRANS
Homo erectus
Australopithecus robustus
Early *Homo habilis*
Early hand-axes

STERKFONTEIN
Homo habilis
Early hand-axes
Australopithecus africanus

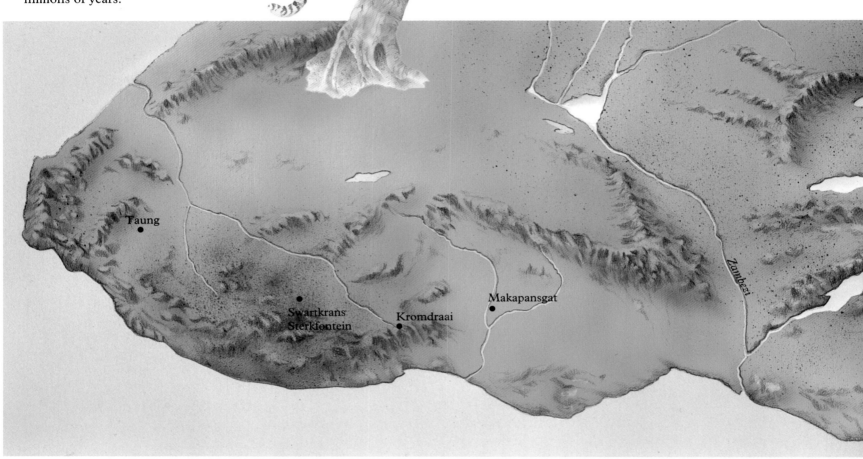

KROMDRAAI
Australopithecus robustus?

MAKAPANSGAT
Australopithecus africanus

LAETOLI
Australopithecus afarensis
(3.7-3.4)

OLDUVAI
Homo erectus? (0.6-0.2)
Homo erectus (1.2-0.8)
Australopithecus boisei (1.7)
Homo habilis (2.2-2.0)
Australopithecus africanus
Simple stone chopping tools

CHESOWANIA
Australopithecus robustus (1.4)

KANAPOI
Homo habilis? (4.0)

LOTHAGAM
Australopithecus? (5.5)

KOOBI FORA
Australopithecus robustus (2.0)
Australopithecus boisei (2.0)
Homo habilis (2.0)

ILERET
Homo erectus (1.5)

LOMEKWI
Australopithecus pre-boisei or
ethiopicus (black skull)
(2.6)

NARIOKOTOME
Homo erectus (1.6)

USNO
Australopithecus africanus

SHUNGURA
Australopithecus africanus
(3.1-2.0)
Australopithecus boisei
(2.2-1.0)

HADAR
Australopithecus afarensis
(Lucy) (3.6)
Homo habilis (3.5)
Simple stone tools (2.5)

5 AUSTRALOPITHECUS AND HOMO HABILIS

Australopithecus afarensis took quite a while to adjust in body and behaviour to the wide open spaces of the savanna, but its skeleton was changing all the time to suit the new conditions. It increased in size, and changes to the backbone and hips allowed these ancient hominids to walk on two legs in a perfectly upright position. They eventually became completely independent of the forest, and this is the stage of evolution that we call *Australopithecus africanus*. A little slimmer than their ancestors, *africanus* were not much more than 130cm (4ft 3in) high and must have weighed 20-30kg (44-66lb).

Africanus and robustus

Fossil remains of *africanus* have been found in deposits in caves and crevices in limestone rocks, together with the bones of animals such as antelopes, jackals, and leopards. We do not know if these remains of *africanus* represented predators or prey, but they certainly ate and were eaten by other animals. They had to be constantly on the look-out for hungry predators, against which they had to defend themselves. They presumably lived in groups, and could use their hands to throw sticks and stones as weapons. Their teeth suggest that their diet was omnivorous, consisting of both plant and animal matter. *Africanus* may have killed some animals, but it is more likely to have simply made use of any dead ones that it found.

Australopithecus africanus lived between three million and one million years ago, and for some of that time lived side by side with some more robust australopithecines. About 2.3 million years ago the climate began to get drier and the vegetation became sparser. The australopithecines, not yet having mastered the art of hunting, had to rely for food largely on underground roots and tubers, together with occasional seed crops.

Food of this kind was tough and not easily digestible,

Reconstruction of a male *Australopithecus africanus*

but one group of australopithecines adapted to it quite well. Their jaws and teeth became larger, and powerful facial muscles allowed them to grind up the food like millstones. These new creatures were *Australopithecus robustus*. They were about 150cm (4ft 11in) tall and weighed about 50kg (110lb), and they were much more suited to life on the dry grasslands.

The first finds of *robustus*, dating from about 1.8 million years ago, were made in South Africa in 1938, while a larger form with a bigger brain was found in Olduvai, in Tanzania, in 1959. This large australopithecine was

The picture below (shown in colour on pages 20/21) is a scene from the daily life of the australopithecines and *Homo habilis*, who lived on the dry grasslands of East Africa, at the edge of the forest, between 2.3 and 1.5 million years ago.

On the left a group of *Australopithecus africanus* are competing with hyenas and vultures for the remains of a dead zebra. Their hands, no longer needed for walking, are able to grasp sticks and stones for use as weapons.

In the centre a few *Australopithecus robustus* are searching for food. They were largely vegetarian and fed mainly on stems, roots, and tubers. This tough food required a more powerful chewing mechanism, as shown by their heavy, protruding jaws. Because of their different feeding habits, *africanus* and *robustus* did not fight over food and they lived peacefully on the savanna.

Homo habilis lived in the same region, but was a more intelligent creature – perhaps the first true human being. *Habilis* could make tools and weapons, and this helped them to get plenty of food. They picked fruit from the forest and dug roots and tubers from the ground (right). Out on the savanna, one group of hunters attacks an antelope, while another cuts up its kill.

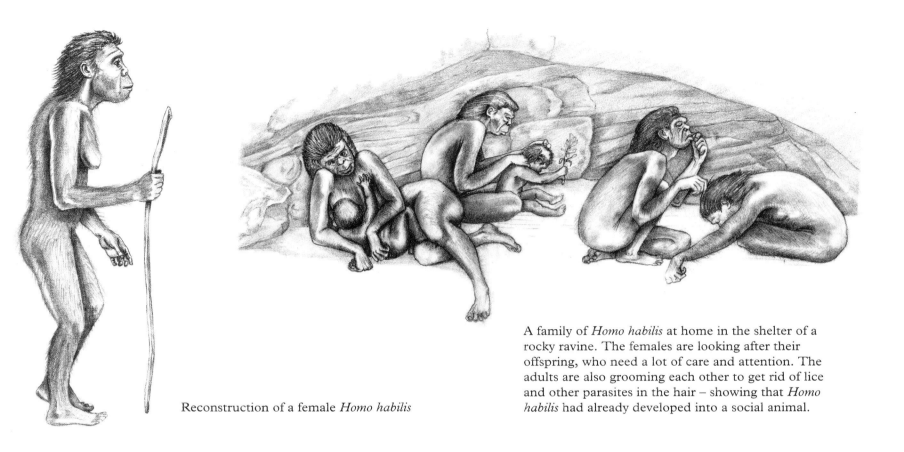

Reconstruction of a female *Homo habilis*

A family of *Homo habilis* at home in the shelter of a rocky ravine. The females are looking after their offspring, who need a lot of care and attention. The adults are also grooming each other to get rid of lice and other parasites in the hair – showing that *Homo habilis* had already developed into a social animal.

originally named *Zinjanthropus boisei*, in honour of Charles Boise who helped to finance the expedition.

Zinjanthropus means 'man of Zinj', which was the old Arabic name for East Africa, but the name has now been dropped and the fossils called *Australopithecus boisei*. The characteristics of *robustus* and *boisei* suggest that they are more closely linked to *afarensis* than to *africanus*, and not particularly close to the main line of human evolution.

'Handy man'

In the Olduvai Gorge in 1961, at a lower level than the *boisei* remains, anthropologists unearthed fragments of a skull with more human characteristics than *boisei*. Although it was older than *boisei*, this skull belonged to a more advanced and presumably more intelligent hominid. Then, two years later, more bones and a few stone tools were found on an even lower level. These tools were simple choppers, with a cutting edge chipped away on one side. The skull discovered in 1961 was named *Homo habilis*, meaning 'handy man'. The term 'man' was used to indicate the human characteristics of the skull, while 'handy' referred to his evident toolmaking skill.

Although *Australopithecus robustus* and *Homo habilis* shared the same open habitat, there was little or no competition for food between them and they almost certainly lived peacefully together along the river banks and the forest edges. *Australopithecus robustus* – and its larger cousin *boisei* – were vegetarians, but *Homo habilis* was omnivorous, just like its ancestor *Australopithecus africanus*. *Australopithecus robustus* was bigger, but *habilis* was more intelligent and was able to make simple tools.

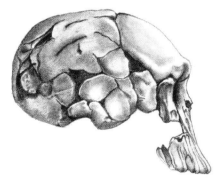

The 2 million-year-old skull of *Homo habilis*, found to the east of Lake Turkana in Kenya. The volume of the cranium (brain case) is 770cc. The brow ridges above the eyes are not particularly large, but there is a marked forward projection of the jaw.

A reconstruction of the brain of *Australopithecus africanus* (left) compared with that of *Homo habilis*. The latter is much bigger and more complex than that of *Australopithecus*, indicating that *Homo habilis* was a more intelligent species.

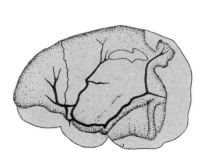
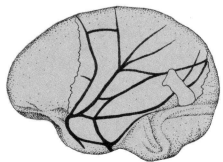

The Tanzanian Highlands were probably the setting for the first human culture. Many important hominid fossils have been found at Olduvai Gorge, about 40km (25 miles) long, where the river has cut deeply into rock layers formed over millions of years.

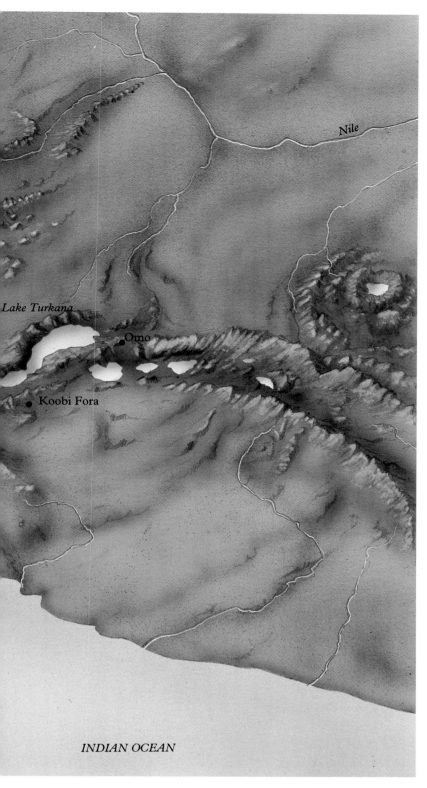

Nile

Lake Turkana

Omo

Koobi Fora

INDIAN OCEAN

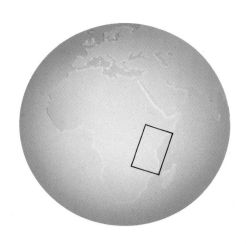

The scene below shows how the Olduvai region might have looked about two million years ago when *Homo habilis* was living there. Below the picture is a map of the Olduvai Basin, showing the many sites where remains of australopithecines and *Homo habilis* have been found.

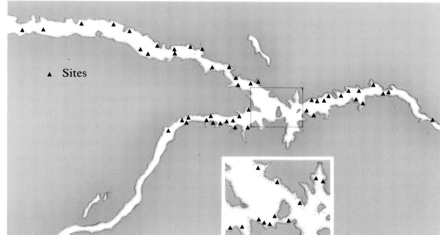

▲ Sites

Australopithecus robustus and the related *Zinjanthropus*, or *Australopithecus, boisei* were vegetarians, with powerful jaws and large cheek teeth to cope with the rather tough vegetation in their dry environment. They may well have been nomads, wandering from place to place and having no settled homes. *Homo habilis* was very different. Descended from a more slender race of australopithecines, they remained slim and became much more upright. Like their ancestors, they were omnivorous and had much smaller teeth than *robustus* and *boisei*, although their jaws were still fairly prominent. But it was the brain of *Homo habilis* that was so different from those of the australopithecines.

Intelligence and speech
A larger brain and greater intelligence enabled *Homo habilis* to make and use simple stone tools, and these enabled them to hunt and to exploit new sources of food. The shape of the inside of *Homo habilis* skulls shows that the region of the brain that we now know is concerned with speech was already quite well developed. So we can be fairly sure that *Homo habilis* could talk. We also know, from discoveries in several parts of East Africa, that *Homo habilis* lived and worked in social groups. This would not have been very easy without some kind of speech.

Family groups
A social group probably consisted of several monogamous family units, each with one man and one woman and their children. As far as we can tell, each group settled in a particular area and stayed there until all the food and other resources of the area had been used up. Everyone had a job to do. The men hunted animals for food and also made most of the tools. The women

Homo habilis walked with a slight stoop, but was completely bipedal, meaning that these ancestors of ours walked entirely on their feet. Their hands, which were already very much like those of present-day people, were very flexible and, aided and controlled by the large brain, could hold and manipulate all kinds of objects.

probably collected fruit and other vegetable food, and also looked after the children and the home. Both sexes may have helped with building the simple shelters of stones and branches.

Homes and tools
Excavations at Olduvai, at the base of rocks dating back

The scene below (pictured in colour on pages 24/25) shows a community of *Homo habilis* on the tree-dotted savanna of the Rift Valley. All the individuals in the community are related to each other, and the work is divided up among them.

On the left, a small group is sitting in the shelter of a

primitive hut and stripping the meat from the carcase of a small animal killed by a hunter. The food will be distributed to all members of the family.

At the foot of a nearby tree, one woman is picking fruit, while another is roughly shaping a block of stone.

In the foreground an older,

more experienced, person shows others how to break stones for making simple axes and knives. The need to teach and learn must have led to the first forms of speech.

Further back in the scene, three people are dividing up a zebra carcase, while another animal is brought into the camp

by two hunters. The river, with its plentiful supply of stones for tool-making, would have been an important factor in deciding where to camp: as well as providing drinking water, the river contained edible plants and fish.

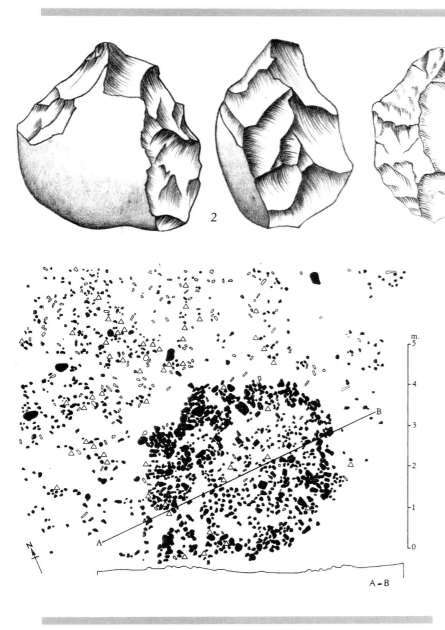

Examples of early stone axes or chopping tools attributed to *Homo habilis* (based on the work of Louis Leakey). The tools were made by chipping flakes away from one or both sides to leave a sharp edge. Tools of this kind have been found at Olduvai and are known as Oldowan tools.

The diagram on the left is of a 1.8 million-year-old settlement, found at Olduvai in 1971. The stone circle (in black) is the remains of a low stone wall that lined the base of a shelter made of branches. Finds of stone choppers and animal bones, marked by triangles, are scattered all around the settlement.

Olduvai, two million years ago. The climate was more humid than now and allowed a huge variety of plants to flourish. The variety of animals was also remarkable, many of them being very similar to today's African animals.
1 *Phacochoerus* – a relative of today's pigs
2 *Homotherium* – a sabre-toothed cat
3 *Sivatherium* – an ancestor of the giraffe
4 A baboon
5 Zebras
6 A chalicothere – a distant relative of the horse
7 An early kind of gazelle
8 A vulture
9 *Dinotherium* – an ancestral elephant

about 1.8 million years, have revealed a circular area of about 16 sq metres (172 sq ft), bordered by a stone circle that had probably been the base of a hut or a shelter made from branches. Inside the circle were the bones of antelopes, giraffes, hippopotamuses, zebras, and other animals. Many of the bones had been broken to extract the nutritious marrow. *Homo habilis* hunted mostly small prey, but they also scavenged for the remains of animals killed by larger predators or by natural causes. The animals were carried back to the camp where, as the numerous bones and stone tools indicate, they were cut up and distributed to all members of the group. Settlements had to be near rocks that would provide the raw materials from which the stone tools could be made.

In order to survive, *Homo habilis* groups had to observe nature closely. They had to learn where useful plants were likely to grow, and understand and predict the movements of animals if they were to get enough food. They also had to know how to defend themselves against large predators, such as lions and leopards. Although weaker than some of the australopithecines with whom they shared the savanna, *habilis*'s intelligence and 'handiness' in making tools and shelters helped them to overcome the challenging and often unfavourable environment.

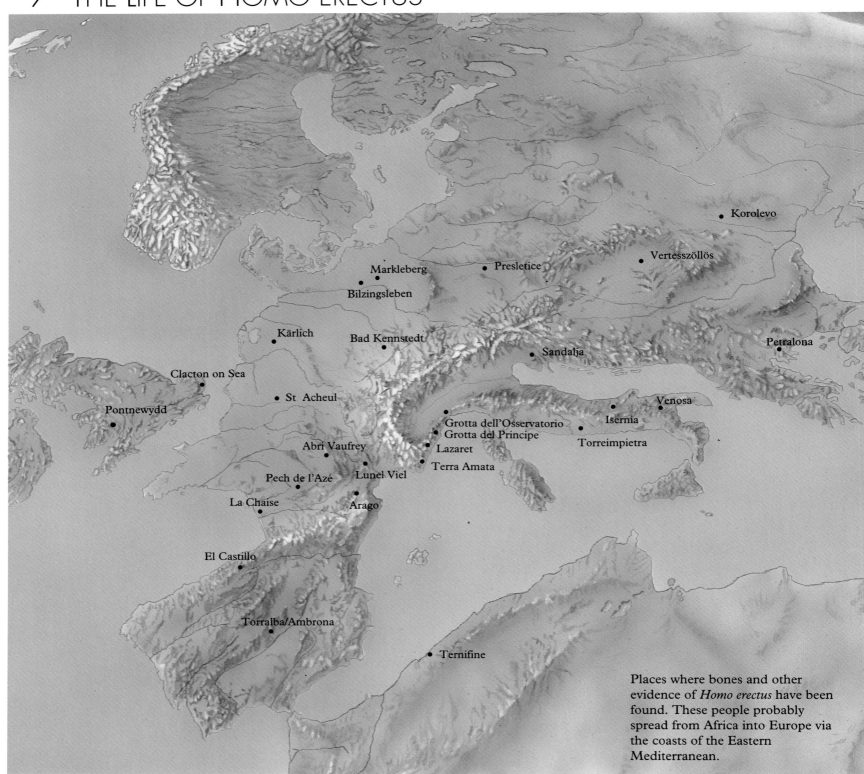

Places where bones and other evidence of *Homo erectus* have been found. These people probably spread from Africa into Europe via the coasts of the Eastern Mediterranean.

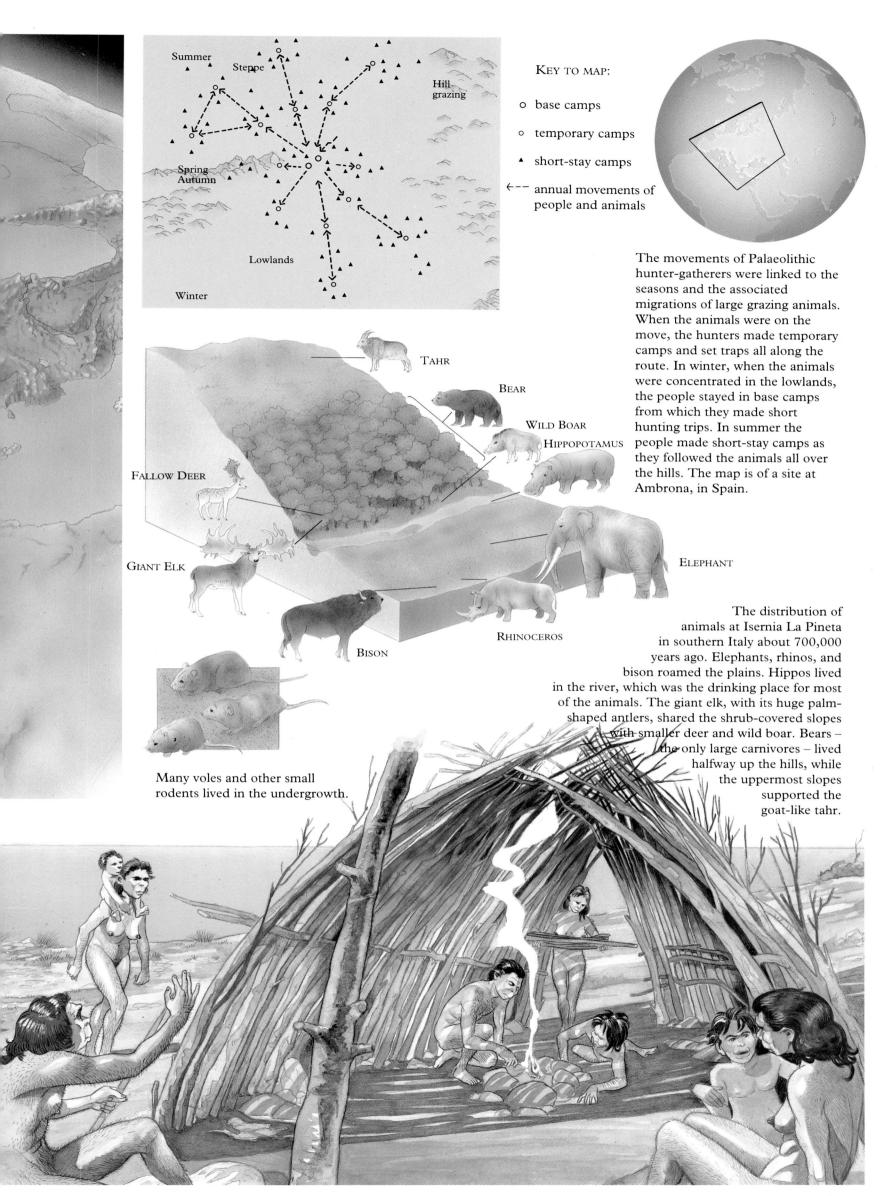

KEY TO MAP:

- ○ base camps
- ○ temporary camps
- ▲ short-stay camps
- ←-- annual movements of people and animals

The movements of Palaeolithic hunter-gatherers were linked to the seasons and the associated migrations of large grazing animals. When the animals were on the move, the hunters made temporary camps and set traps all along the route. In winter, when the animals were concentrated in the lowlands, the people stayed in base camps from which they made short hunting trips. In summer the people made short-stay camps as they followed the animals all over the hills. The map is of a site at Ambrona, in Spain.

TAHR

BEAR

WILD BOAR

HIPPOPOTAMUS

FALLOW DEER

GIANT ELK

ELEPHANT

BISON

RHINOCEROS

The distribution of animals at Isernia La Pineta in southern Italy about 700,000 years ago. Elephants, rhinos, and bison roamed the plains. Hippos lived in the river, which was the drinking place for most of the animals. The giant elk, with its huge palm-shaped antlers, shared the shrub-covered slopes with smaller deer and wild boar. Bears – the only large carnivores – lived halfway up the hills, while the uppermost slopes supported the goat-like tahr.

Many voles and other small rodents lived in the undergrowth.

7 THE LIFE OF HOMO ERECTUS

Homo habilis succeeded in the relatively hostile environment of the savanna thanks to its superior brain power and its ability to manipulate the environment to its own advantage. The biological and cultural evolution that started with *Homo habilis* accelerated rapidly, and about two million years ago – barely half a million years after the appearance of *Homo habilis* – a new hominid arrived on the scene. This was *Homo erectus*, who had a taller forehead and a larger brain case than *Homo habilis*, and a broad, forward-jutting face with large cheek teeth. The skeleton was heavier than that of *Homo habilis* and the average height was 160-170cm (5ft 3in–5ft 7in). *Homo erectus* was not really much more erect or upright than *Homo habilis*, but when it was first discovered – in Java in 1891 – it was the only known upright fossil hominid. Originally called *Pithecanthropus erectus*, meaning 'upright ape-man', the skeleton shows that the creature was a true human and thus belongs in the genus *Homo*.

The evolution from *Homo habilis* to *Homo erectus* took place in very small steps and the two species graded into each other, so it is not possible to say exactly when *habilis* became *erectus*. The remains of *Homo erectus* settlements in widely scattered places, such as Olduvai in Tanzania, Melka Kunturé in Ethiopia, and Terra Amata in France, show that many cultural changes took place alongside the physical ones as *Homo erectus* evolved from *Homo habilis*.

A reconstruction of *Homo erectus*, carrying a burning brand and a hunting stick or spear.

Using fire

The most important cultural change arose from the discovery of fire – a discovery that completely changed the life of *Homo erectus*. It was probably a natural event, such as an erupting volcano or a tree set on fire by lightning, that aroused human interest in this mysterious element, but the conquest of fire signalled an enormous step forward. Fire kept people warm and protected them from predatory animals. It also enabled them to harden the points of their spears or hunting sticks, and it meant that they could cook their food. Because cooking makes many foods easier to digest, people were able to eat a wider range of plants than their ancestors. Cooking, and the reduction in the need for prolonged chewing, may even have led to the smaller jaws of later humans.

Living together

Homo erectus lived in small groups, the size of which would have been linked to the resources of the territory.

The picture below appears in colour on pages 28/29. *Homo erectus* spent several weeks each year in a coastal settlement at Terra Amata, where Nice is today. The hunting was good, and an animal carcase can be seen being brought into camp by the hunters on the left.

In the foreground, two men are making various stone tools with the new bifacial method, in which flakes are chipped from both sides of the stone. They are making tools for cutting, scraping, and carving. Next to them, a hunter has finished hardening and pointing his spear in the fire. Behind him, two women are looking after their children.

The group spent quite long periods in these 'base camps', and built quite solid dwellings with wood and bone covered with branches and animal skins. *Homo erectus* used fire to keep warm and to keep predators away, as well as for cooking food. With plenty of plants and animals around, they were not short of food. Life was quite comfortable for *Homo erectus* here on the shores of the Mediterranean.

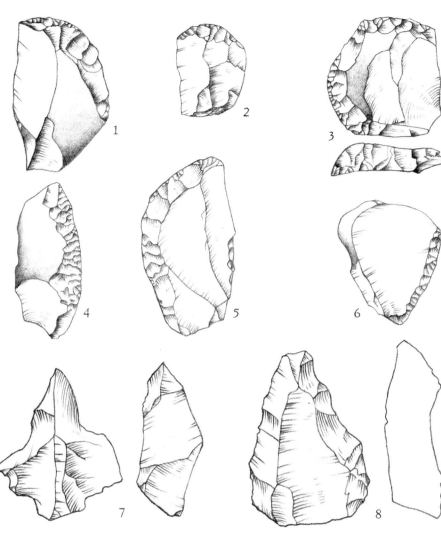

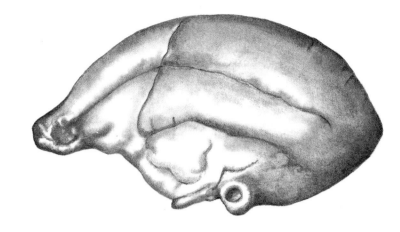

A reconstruction of part of a skull of *Pithecanthropus erectus*, found at Sangiran on the island of Java in 1937. *Pithecanthropus* was later classified as *Homo erectus*.

On the left is a selection of Acheulean stone tools:
1-3 scrapers
4-6 rasps
7 a boring tool or perhaps a spear-head
8 a rasp

The Oldowan pebble tool culture, the world's oldest industry, started in the lower part of the Palaeolithic, or Old Stone Age, with simple chopping tools. These fist-sized tools were attributed mainly to *Homo habilis*.

The choppers gradually developed into hand-axes, made from stones that were worked on both sides to produce straight cutting edges. Tools of this kind are referred to as Acheulean, from St Acheul in France where many have been found. Produced by *Homo erectus*, some of them are beautifully symmetrical and show that people were already taking a pride in their work. Acheulean tools also include rasps, scrapers, and carving tools.

The tools were initially made by striking one stone with another, but *Homo erectus* began to use bone and horn, and even wood to shape the stones. This method, known as the Levalloisian technique, produced thin flakes. The edges were very sharp and the tools were much more efficient cutters than the earlier hand-axes. Levalloisian tools mark the transition from the lower to the middle Old Stone Age.

Each group probably contained several family units and they probably stayed in one place for quite a while, especially when looking after babies. They built huts with branches or with larger timber. They also used large bones for building, and covered the huts with animal skins. The stone circles that have been discovered in many places may have been the bases of the huts. The circles contain stone tools, animal bones, and also the remains of fires.

When the resources of a territory were exhausted, the group moved to another area with plenty of game and vegetation, but their settlements had to be near rivers and also near rocks from which to get the raw materials for their tools. The stone tools did not last very long and they were always making new ones. Groups also moved on a seasonal basis, following the animal herds to lower and warmer areas for the winter.

Improved toolmaking techniques

The stone tool industry was being improved all the time and the tools of *Homo erectus* were very much better than the hand-choppers that *Homo habilis* left at Olduvai. One of the most important tools was the hand-axe, a pear-shaped instrument worked on both sides to give a sharp cutting edge. The early hand-axes were fairly rough, but as techniques improved for chipping flakes away from the stones they became more elegant – and also much sharper and more efficient. Knives, chisels, and various forms of scrapers were also made with the new techniques.

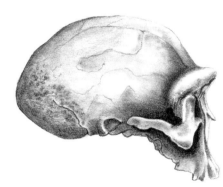

The skull of *Homo erectus* from Koobi Fora in Kenya. It is about 1.5 million years old.

Below are some hand-axes from Terra Amata, skilfully made using the bifacial method, taken from the work of H. de Lumley.

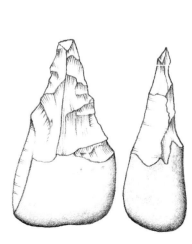

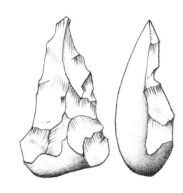

8 HOMO ERECTUS CONQUERS THE OLD WORLD

About one and a half million years ago *Homo erectus* began to spread across the Old World. Coming from East Africa, they probably first reached western Asia and from there spread all over Europe and across Asia to China and Indonesia. Over many generations, they became adapted to the different climates and habitats – from the cold of the Ice Age tundra to the warm coasts and heat of India's tropical forests. The map (right) shows important sites where evidence of *Homo erectus* has been found.

Some 450,000 years ago, in a place not far from present-day Beijing in China, the Choukoutien Cave on the Hill of the Dragon's Teeth was used as a shelter by *Homo erectus*. The collapse of the roof about 300,000 years ago greatly reduced the size of the accommodation and forced the inhabitants to move to the western part of the cave, which was entered through a central fissure.

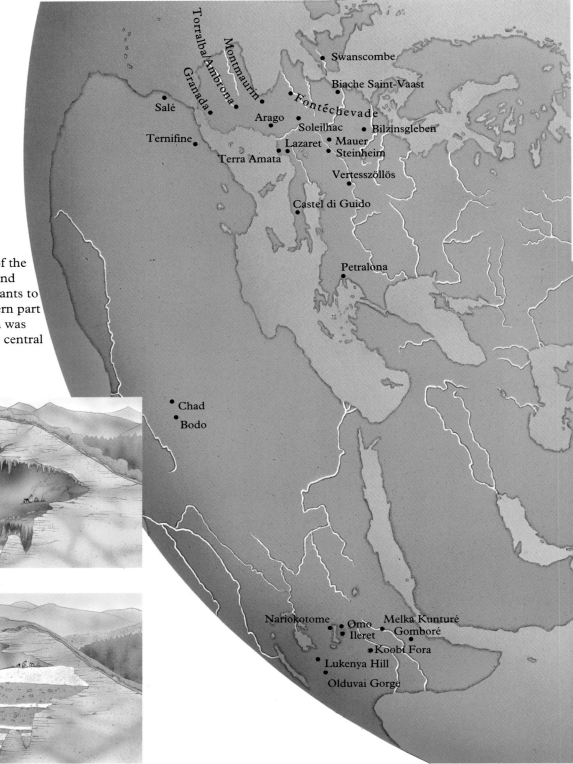

Torralba/Ambrona
Montmaurin
Granada
Swanscombe
Salé
Biache Saint-Vaast
Arago
Fontéchevade
Soleilhac
Bilzinsgleben
Ternifine
Lazaret
Mauer
Steinheim
Terra Amata
Vertesszöllös
Castel di Guido
Petralona
Chad
Bodo
Nariokotome
Omo
Melka Kunturé
Ileret
Gomboré
Koobi Fora
Lukenya Hill
Olduvai Gorge

The increasingly more efficient use of the resources in an area, such as East Africa's Rift Valley, that accompanied the advances in tool-making and greater co-operation between family groups inevitably led to better food supplies and population increases. As the populations increased, the hunting parties were forced to go further afield to find food, and if they found particularly good hunting areas it is likely that some families in a settlement would have moved permanently into these new areas.

This process could well have been repeated by every generation.

The diagram on the right shows how small groups of people may have split away from their settlements and followed the herds of grazing animals in search of more open hunting grounds. Limited by large rivers and mountain ranges, they all had to follow the same routes and the groups inevitably met up from time to time. They may well have joined forces and settled down to form new communities – until population increases led to new cycles of emigration.

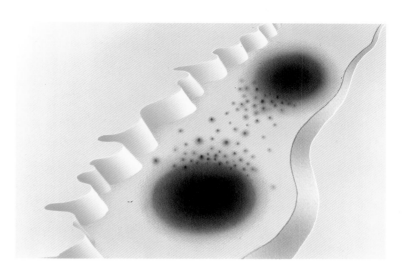

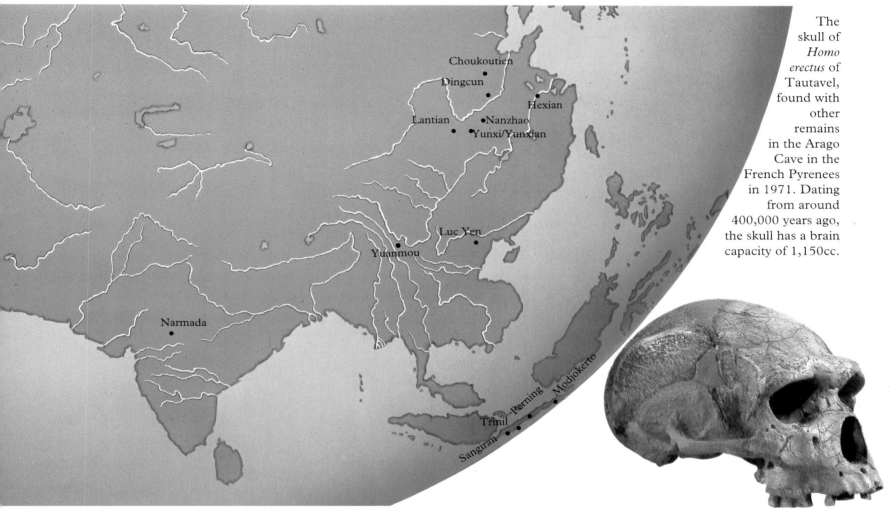

The skull of *Homo erectus* of Tautavel, found with other remains in the Arago Cave in the French Pyrenees in 1971. Dating from around 400,000 years ago, the skull has a brain capacity of 1,150cc.

8 HOMO ERECTUS CONQUERS THE OLD WORLD

About one and a half million years ago, *Homo erectus* began to spread out from their original home in Africa's Rift Valley. The reason for the rather sudden spread of this close ancestor of modern humans was rapid increases in population associated with better living conditions – themselves the result of discovering fire and making better and more efficient tools and hunting equipment. As the populations increased, many groups, probably made up of young people, moved away to seek food supplies in new areas.

From Africa to Asia

After reaching North Africa, one group of these Stone Age people spread eastwards into Asia. We do not know much about the route they took, but we do know that they settled in the Narmada Valley in India, where some 600,000-year-old remains have been found.

China's most famous site for fossil humans is the village of Choukoutien, not far from Beijing (Peking). On the Hill of the Dragon's Teeth there are many caves that were occupied by people more than 450,000 years ago, and continued to be occupied for more than 200,000 years. The site got its name because of the many teeth that workers found there while quarrying the limestone. The teeth belonged to people not to dragons. Skulls and other bones were also found. The name *Sinanthropus pekinensis*, or Peking Man, was originally coined for these remains, but they are now classed with all the other human fossils of similar age as *Homo erectus*. But Peking Man is not the oldest example in China. A 600,000-year-old skull was found at Lantian, and several 700,000-year-old teeth have been unearthed at Yuanmou.

Some of the migrants who went to Asia ended up in Indonesia, which was then still connected to the mainland of Asia. A skull with a mixture of human and ape-

On the right are some simple stone chopping tools from Choukoutien.

As well as cooking with fire and frightening away wild beasts, *Homo erectus* heated wooden weapons and utensils to harden them.

like features was discovered at Trinil, in Java, in 1891, and the next year a typically human thigh bone was found just a few metres away. It was not known at the time whether these remains belonged to an ape or a hominid, and they were called *Pithecanthropus erectus*, meaning 'upright ape-man'. Many other remains have been discovered since, some about 1.2 million years old. It soon became clear that they belonged to early humans, and they are all now known as *Homo erectus*.

From Africa to Europe

Another group of *Homo erectus* invaded Europe, probably

The cave of Choukoutien (pictured in colour on pages 32/33) was a permanent home for *Homo erectus* for thousands of years. Here, and in many of the other places in which they settled as they spread across Europe and Asia, the ability to make fire was a great help. Much social life was probably centred on the fire, as it is in many households today.

A large group has gathered around the fire on the left to listen to one of their members describing a hunting trip or some other experience. Many hand gestures would have accompanied the simple language.

In the centre of the picture, two hunters are checking the points of their hunting spears, which they have hardened in the fire. Three other hunters have arrived with a dead antelope and are calling for help. The man with the lighted torch will guide them into the cave.

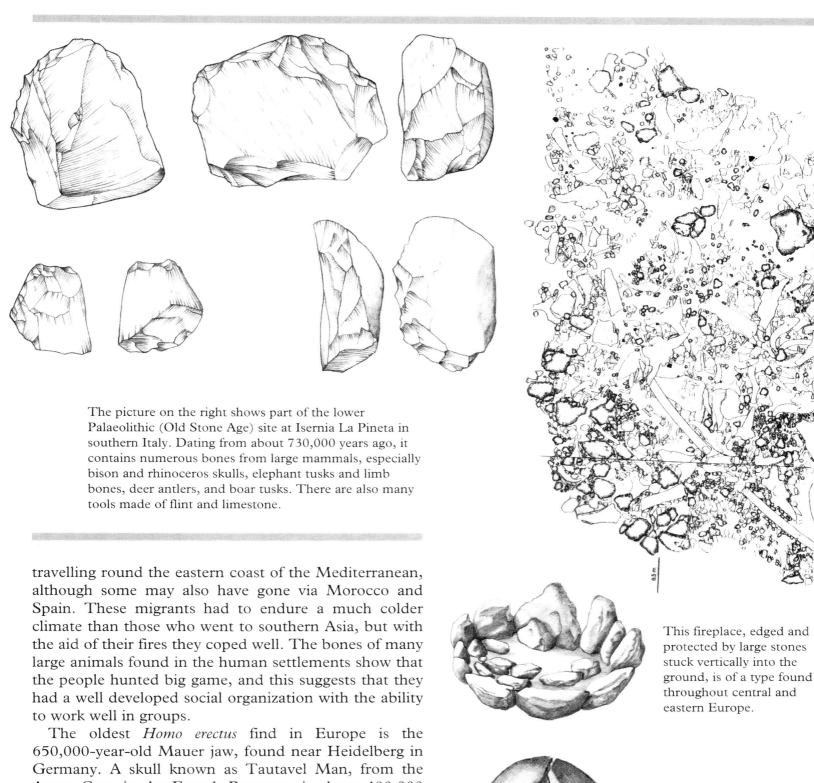

The picture on the right shows part of the lower Palaeolithic (Old Stone Age) site at Isernia La Pineta in southern Italy. Dating from about 730,000 years ago, it contains numerous bones from large mammals, especially bison and rhinoceros skulls, elephant tusks and limb bones, deer antlers, and boar tusks. There are also many tools made of flint and limestone.

travelling round the eastern coast of the Mediterranean, although some may also have gone via Morocco and Spain. These migrants had to endure a much colder climate than those who went to southern Asia, but with the aid of their fires they coped well. The bones of many large animals found in the human settlements show that the people hunted big game, and this suggests that they had a well developed social organization with the ability to work well in groups.

The oldest *Homo erectus* find in Europe is the 650,000-year-old Mauer jaw, found near Heidelberg in Germany. A skull known as Tautavel Man, from the Arago Cave in the French Pyrenees, is about 400,000 years old, while Vertesszöllös Man, found near Budapest in Hungary, had a larger skull and lived perhaps 300,000 years ago. From the Petralona Cave in northern Greece comes a skull whose age is in dispute. Some scientists estimate that it is about 600,000 years old, while others put its age at no more than about 200,000 years. A 500,000-year-old bone from Boxgrove in Sussex, England, may belong to *Homo erectus*, as may remains from Atapuerca, Spain. Definite *erectus* finds in Europe are rarer than other signs of their presence. Terra Amata, a beautiful site now occupied by the French city of Nice, was inhabited by Stone Age hunters 400,000 years ago and, as well as their stone tools, they left traces of a fireplace and a single human footprint. At Isernia La Pineta, in southern Italy, stone tools and animal bones have been found in the remains of a temporary settlement used for hunting about 730,000 years ago.

This fireplace, edged and protected by large stones stuck vertically into the ground, is of a type found throughout central and eastern Europe.

A nodule of pyrites (iron sulphide) from the Chaleux Cave at Dinat in Belgium. Striking this shiny mineral produces sparks, which Stone-Age people could have used to start fires with the help of dry moss and twigs.

Rotating a stick rapidly in a hole in a piece of wood was another way of starting fires. The over-heated wood would readily ignite dry grass and twigs.

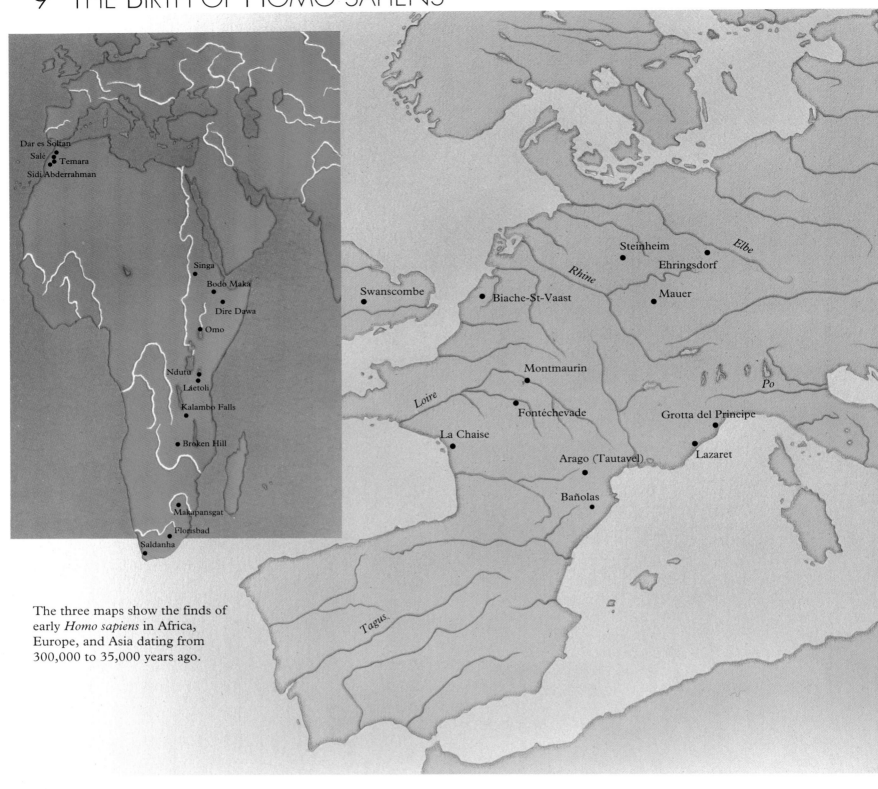

The three maps show the finds of early *Homo sapiens* in Africa, Europe, and Asia dating from 300,000 to 35,000 years ago.

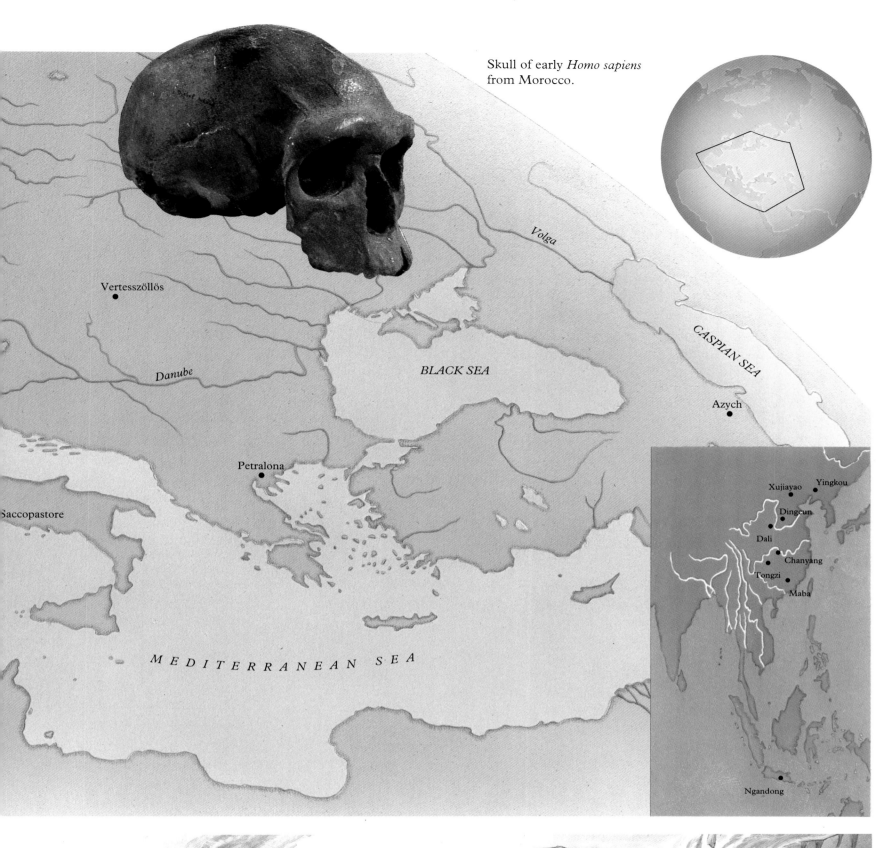

Skull of early *Homo sapiens* from Morocco.

Vertesszöllös

Volga

Danube

BLACK SEA

CASPIAN SEA

Azych

Saccopastore

Petralona

MEDITERRANEAN SEA

Xujiayao   Yingkou

Dingcun

Dali

Chanyang

Tongzi

Maba

Ngandong

9 The Birth of Homo sapiens

The spread of *Homo erectus* across the Old World was a remarkable event, although the numbers involved were actually quite small to start with. Probably only a million individuals left Africa's Rift Valley, and a million years later (500,000 years ago) there were probably only about 10 million of them. Human remains are rather rare although, thanks to intensive excavation, they have been discovered over a wide area and a wide range of geological time. Traces of settlements, with stone tools and animal bones, are much more common and have been found throughout Africa and Eurasia.

Huge areas of Europe and northern Asia were covered by ice-age glaciers on several occasions, and there are obviously no traces of human life from those areas at those times, although people did manage to live around the edges of the ice sheets.

Our species evolved

After leaving the Rift Valley, *Homo erectus* continued to evolve and slowly gave rise to more modern human beings. But they were not all alike. Separated by ice, seas, and mountains as they spread into different areas, the various populations of *Homo erectus* evolved in different ways. Some became adapted to warm climates and some to cooler environments, and they looked quite different from each other. By about 250,000 years ago, the Old World was populated with races halfway between the original *Homo erectus* and present-day people. These new races were the first *Homo sapiens* – the species to which we ourselves belong.

In Europe there was Steinheim Man, known from a 200,000-year-old skull found in Germany, and in Asia there was Solo Man, up to 250,000 years old, known from 13 skulls found in the Solo River valley in Java. In Africa there was Rhodesian Man, whose skull was found

Right: a double-edged spear-head of the late Acheulean culture (Lower Palaeolithic), found near Bologna in Italy.

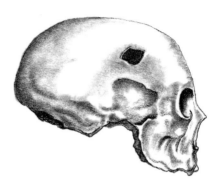

A reconstruction of the head of an early male *Homo sapiens*.

A woman's skull found at Saccopastore, near Rome, in 1925. Associated with Mousterian tools, it is about 100,000 years old, from a period before that of typical Neanderthal people. The brain case had a capacity of 1,200cc.

at Broken Hill in what is now Zambia. Rhodesian Man lived between 100,000 and 40,000 years ago.

Hunting together

Technical skills were changing as well as the physical appearance of the Stone-Age people. The design of the Acheulean hand-axes became more refined as new techniques for chipping the stones were discovered. The

This group of early *Homo sapiens* (pictured in colour on pages 36/37) take part in big-game hunting, an activity requiring quite complex group organization and familiarity with the environment.

One member of the group has been killed by a sabre-toothed cat, which has now been surrounded. The men are attacking it with force and each one has his own task. The two on the left are hurling stones at

the beast, and another has just thrown his spear, its point hardened by fire. Other men are using fire and spears to attack the cat, and the man on the right is keeping them supplied with lighted branches.

The group's actions are all well co-ordinated because the people have developed a working language: their lives depend on it.

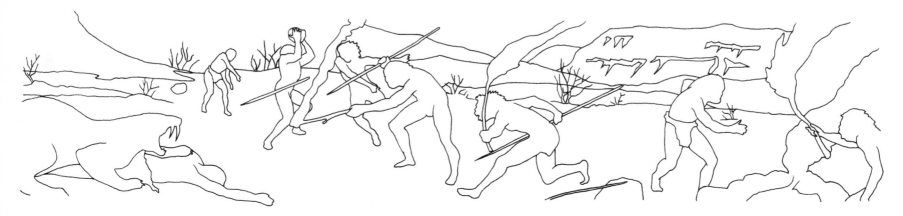

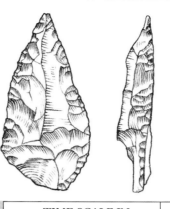
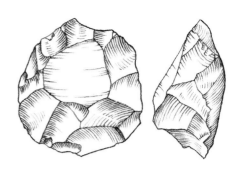

A Mousterian spear-head, bound into a notch at the tip of the spear (below left), and a wooden point from Clacton-on-Sea in England (below right).

A Mousterian point (seen face- and side-on, right), used as a knife, and a circular core (also seen face- and side-on, far right) from which various points and other small tools have been flaked away.

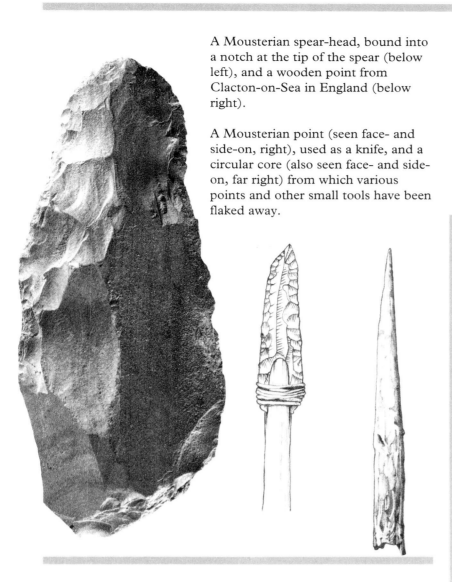

TIME SCALE IN THOUSANDS OF YEARS				WESTERN EUROPE	MIDDLE EAST
Upper Pleistocene	Post-Glacial	8	Upper Palaeolithic		
	Upper Würm Glaciation			Magdalenian	Magdalenian
				Solutrean	Eastern Gravettian
				Perigordian	
				Aurignacian	Aurignacian
		35		Chatelperronian	Szeletian
	Lower Würm Glaciation		Middle Palaeolithic	Mousterian	
		80			
	Riss-Würm Interglacial	120		Pre-Mousterian	
Middle Pleistocene	Riss Glaciation			Upper Acheulean	
		250			Tayacian / Clactonian
	Mindel-Riss Interglacial	300		Middle Acheulean	
	Mindel Glaciation		Lower Palaeolithic	Lower Acheulean	
		650			
	Gunz-Mindel Interglacial	700			
Lower Pleistocene	Gunz Glaciation	1200		Pebble Culture (Oldowan)	
	Donau-Gunz Interglacial	1800			

Levalloisian system, involving the removal of thin flakes by applying pressure right at the edge of the stone, produced a wide range of delicate cutting and scraping tools, many of which were very attractive.

Now that they had the right tools and weapons, *Homo sapiens* could hunt big game, an activity requiring properly co-ordinated group action. The hunting areas had to be surveyed so that the animals' movements could be predicted, and plans had to be drawn up for approaching and surrounding the animals before moving in for the kill. All this would have necessitated advanced levels of communication and social organization.

The importance of fire

By this time, human society was developing a definite structure. Many families probably lived in caves, especially in the cooler areas, but the people could also build dwellings of various kinds. Separate areas were used for sleeping, eating, and working, and fire was an essential part of everyday life. As well as cooking people's food and giving them warmth, it provided protection against predators and was also used for sharpening and hardening the points of hunting spears. Fires were also used to drive wild animals over precipices or into marshes or blind passages where they could be attacked with rocks and spears.

The importance of fire in people's social and intellectual development should not be forgotten. Family bonds would have been reinforced while sitting around the fire in the evening, and spiritual or even religious beliefs may well have developed at this time.

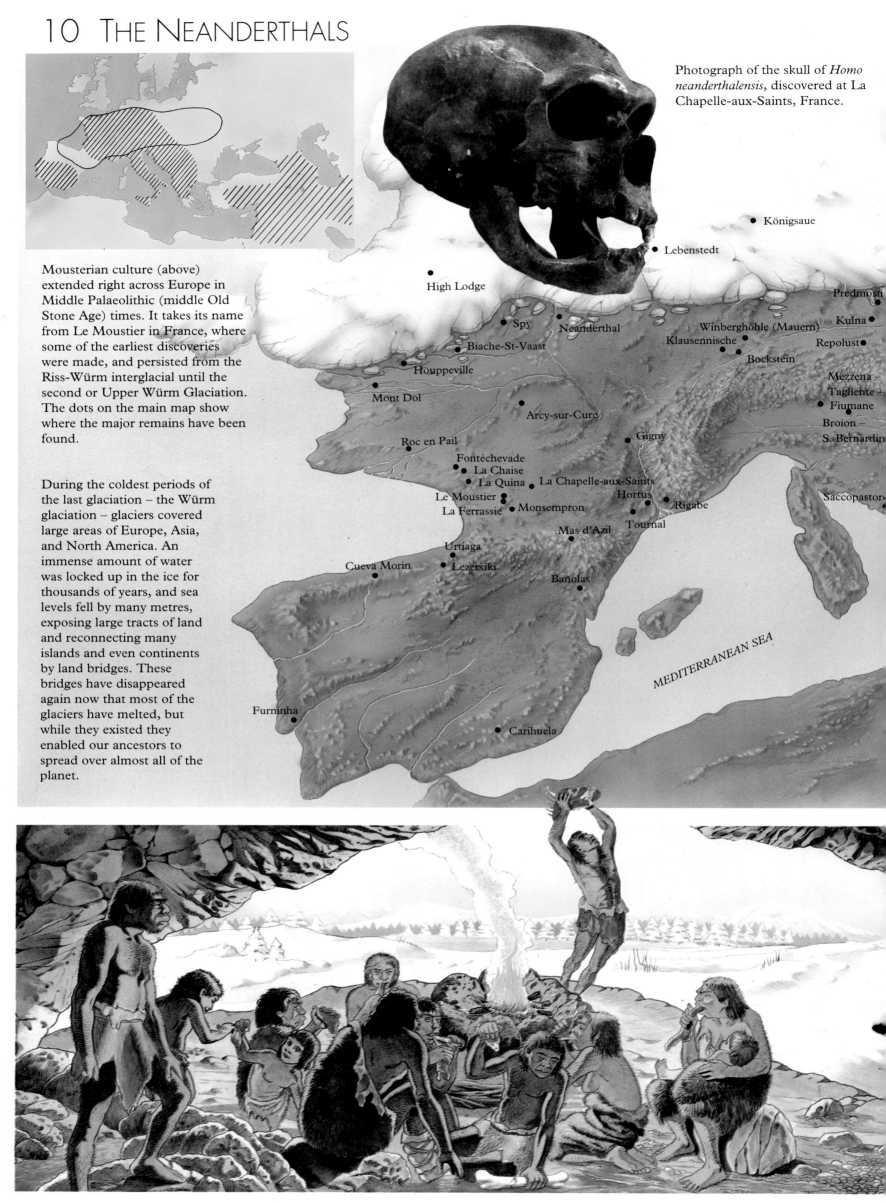

Photograph of the skull of *Homo neanderthalensis*, discovered at La Chapelle-aux-Saints, France.

Mousterian culture (above) extended right across Europe in Middle Palaeolithic (middle Old Stone Age) times. It takes its name from Le Moustier in France, where some of the earliest discoveries were made, and persisted from the Riss-Würm interglacial until the second or Upper Würm Glaciation. The dots on the main map show where the major remains have been found.

During the coldest periods of the last glaciation – the Würm glaciation – glaciers covered large areas of Europe, Asia, and North America. An immense amount of water was locked up in the ice for thousands of years, and sea levels fell by many metres, exposing large tracts of land and reconnecting many islands and even continents by land bridges. These bridges have disappeared again now that most of the glaciers have melted, but while they existed they enabled our ancestors to spread over almost all of the planet.

Königsaue

Lebenstedt

High Lodge

Predmosti

Spy

Neanderthal

Winberghöhle (Mauern)

Kulna

Biache-St-Vaast

Klausennische

Repolust

Bockstein

Houppeville

Mezzena –
Tagliente –
Fiumane

Mont Dol

Arcy-sur-Cure

Broion –
S. Bernardin

Roc en Pail

Gigny

Fontéchevade

La Chaise

La Quina

La Chapelle-aux-Saints

Le Moustier

Hortus

Saccopastor

La Ferrassie

Monsempron

Rigabe

Mas d'Azil

Tournal

Urtiaga

Lezetxiki

Cueva Morin

Bañolas

MEDITERRANEAN SEA

Furninha

Carihuela

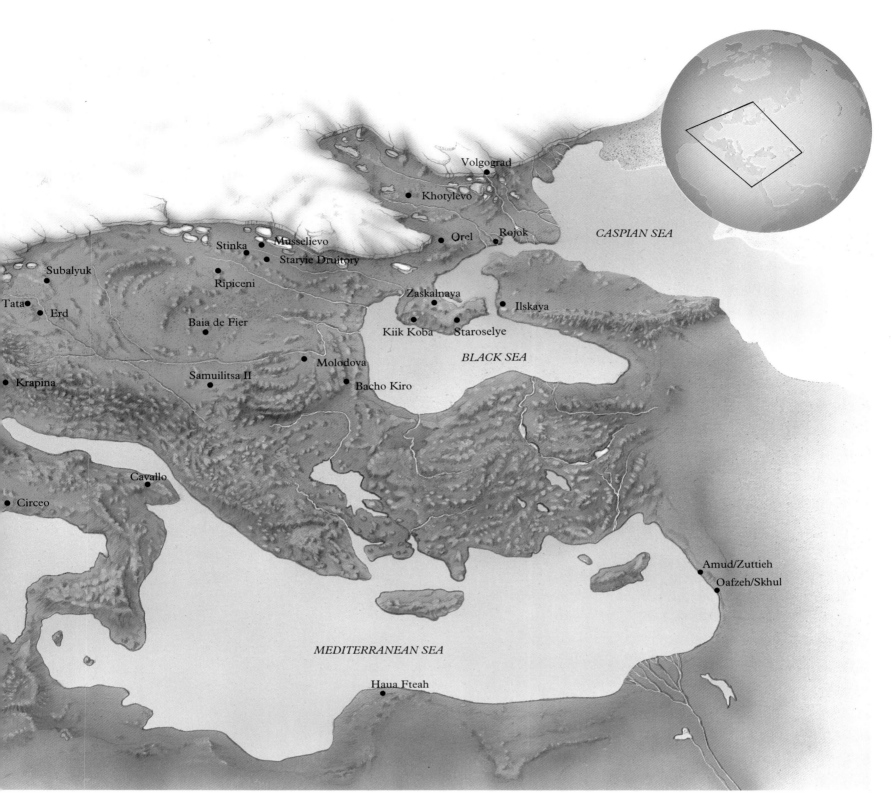

CASPIAN SEA

Volgograd

Khotylevo

Orel
Rojok
Stinka
Musselievo
Staryie Druitory
Subalyuk
Ripiceni
Tata
Erd
Zaskalnaya
Ilskaya
Baia de Fier
Kiik Koba
Staroselye
BLACK SEA
Molodova
Krapina
Samuilitsa II
Bacho Kiro
Cavallo
Amud/Zuttieh
Qafzeh/Skhul
Circeo
MEDITERRANEAN SEA
Haua Fteah

10 THE NEANDERTHALS

The evolutionary path from *Homo erectus* to *Homo sapiens* was gradual and rather irregular, with both biological and cultural changes happening at different speeds in different regions. And not every part of the body evolved at the same rate. For example, a 130,000-year-old skull found in the Omo Valley of Ethiopia could have been classed as *Homo erectus* if observed from the front, but from the rear it is more like *Homo sapiens*.

Short-lived Neanderthals

At about this time, evolution began to produce a stocky, barrel-chested race with short legs and forearms and a bulging face with prominent brow-ridges. These were Neanderthal men and women, who lived over a wide area of Europe and Asia between 100,000 and 35,000 years ago. The Neanderthals seem to us ugly, and it was hard to believe that they were the ancestors of modern human beings. They are now treated as a distinct species – *Homo neanderthalensis* – that branched away from the main line of human evolution and then became extinct without leaving any descendants.

Neanderthals got their name because the first remains of this type were found in 1856 in a cave in the Neander Valley in Germany, although their culture is called Mousterian because many of their stone tools have been found at Le Moustier in France. Neanderthal fossils have also been found in Spain and Belgium, and all the way across to Uzbekistan in Central Asia.

Surviving the cold

Neanderthals took their first steps at the end of the Riss-Würm interglacial, a period with a warm-temperate climate that caused the ice-caps and glaciers to melt. But at the beginning of the Würm glaciation the climate turned cold again and the ice-caps expanded once more. The southern half of Europe remained free of ice, but it was still very cold and the Neanderthals needed

A reconstruction of a Neanderthal woman (left), showing the characteristically bulging face and the prominent brow ridges above the eyes. The stocky build was an adaptation to the cold climate in which the Neanderthals lived.

The jaw of a cave bear (below), complete with its canine tooth, was used as a weapon by the Neanderthals to kill other bears.

all their skills to survive in the hostile environment. Discoveries of their tools and the remains of their fires show that many of them lived in caves – especially in the Dordogne region of France – but other groups camped on flat, open areas.

The most spectacular discovery as far as dwellings are concerned was on the bank of the River Dnieper in Ukraine. It consisted of the remains of an oval hut, about 10 metres (33ft) across, built from mammoth

The scene below (pictured in colour on pages 40/41) depicts the daily life of a small group of Neanderthals living somewhere in central Europe. On the left, among some rocks at the entrance to a cave, they are roasting and eating pieces of a recently killed young mammoth. The boy in the foreground is crushing a bone to suck out the nourishing marrow. Another boy is holding a piece of meat high in the air: is he playing, or is he giving thanks for the meal?

Outside the cave, the mammoth is skilfully butchered by the hunters: a large part of the meat will be buried in the snow to keep it in good condition for a long time.

On the right, in the most sheltered part of the cave, a young woman, killed in an accident or by an unknown illness, is buried in a carefully chosen spot. Ibex horns are placed nearby for ritual or magical purposes.

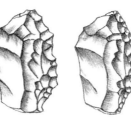

A Levalloisian core.

The core after removal of the principal chip or flake.

Numerous small flakes are removed from the edge of the chip to produce a rasp.

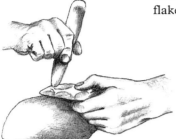

Repeated striking of the edge of the chip . . .

. . . with a piece of wood or bone or another stone . . .

. . . removes flakes from the edges to produce a variety of tools (below).

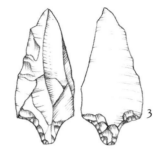

1   2   3   4

THE LEVALLOISIAN TECHNOLOGY OF THE MIDDLE PALAEOLITHIC

Flint was the main stone used for Mousterian tools, and it was worked by the Levalloisian technique, named after the Parisian suburb where this kind of work was first discovered. A rounded stone, known as a core, was roughly shaped by hammering until it had a sharp and rather wavy edge. Further hammering removed slender chips or flakes from the edge. These chips were then worked on with wooden, bone, or stone strikers to remove smaller flakes from the edges and convert them into knives, saws, scrapers, spear heads, and various other tools.

These stone tools (left) were made by the Aterian people of North Africa during middle Palaeolithic times. Their culture and tools were of the Mousterian type and much like those of the Neanderthals in Europe, but they may also have invented the bow and arrow.

1 and 2: Mousterian points, used as knives or scrapers.
3 and 4: spear heads or arrow heads.

---

bones and well preserved in a thick layer of river mud. The hut was probably covered with animal skins when it was in use.

Fighting for food

The Neanderthals were hunter-gatherers, but the proportions of plant and animal food in their diets must have varied with the places in which they lived. The warmer areas in the south would have provided more fruit and other vegetable food than the colder lands around the edges of the ice. Hunting was a major activity of the Neanderthals in Europe and was carried out in groups. Their prey included the horse (200kg or 440lb of meat), the primitive ox, the woolly bison (540kg or 1188lb), and the ibex (30-40kg or 66-88lb). They also hunted young mammoths, and they had to fight cave-bears for possession of their caves.

Burying the dead

Tools and weapons were made of stone and bone. Flint, jasper, and quartz were the main stones used for tool-making, and camps were usually sited within easy reach of good sources of these stones. The first proper burials were undertaken at about this time. The dead were covered in red ochre and set out on a bed of flowers, together with symbolic offerings of meat, eggs, tools, and weapons. The first discovery of such a burial, at La Chapelle-aux-Saints, revealed a skeleton lying in a huddled position in a grave 1.45m (4ft 9in) long, 1m (3ft 3in) wide, and almost 30cm (1ft) deep.

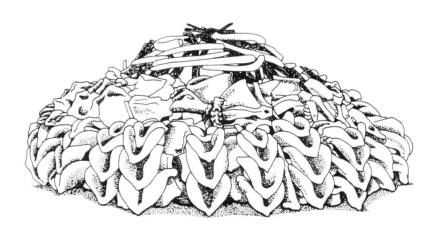

Reconstruction of a hut built with mammoth bones at Mezirici in Ukraine. The walls were made from the massive jaw-bones.

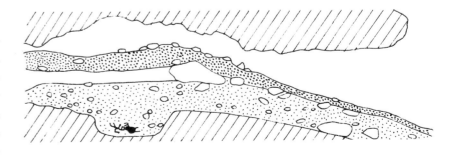

A longitudinal section through the cave of La Chapelle-aux-Saints in France, showing Neanderthal burial sites.

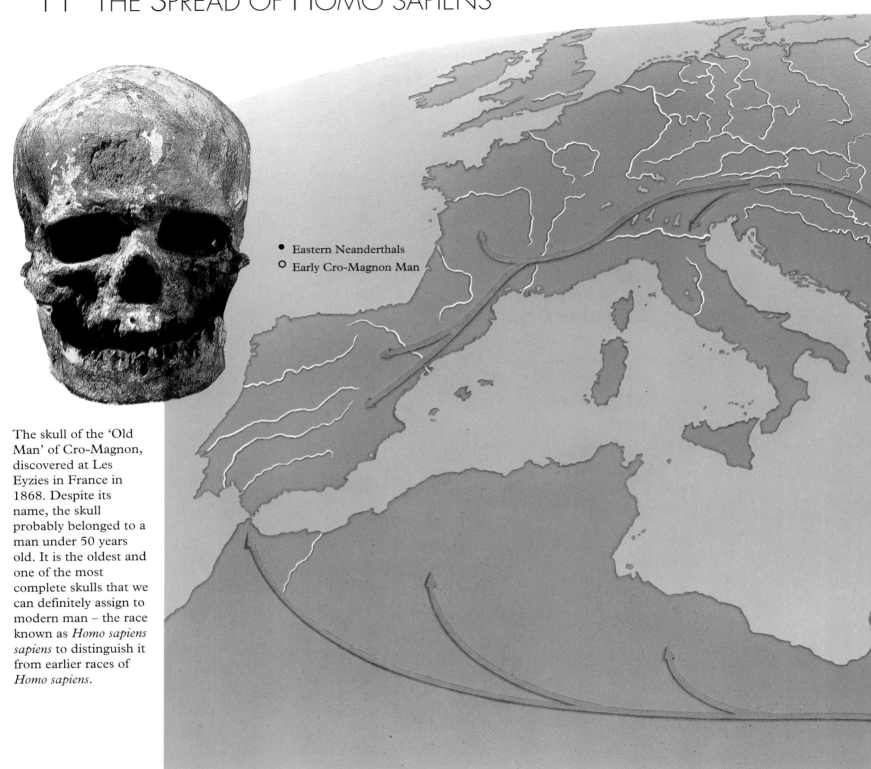

● Eastern Neanderthals
○ Early Cro-Magnon Man

The skull of the 'Old Man' of Cro-Magnon, discovered at Les Eyzies in France in 1868. Despite its name, the skull probably belonged to a man under 50 years old. It is the oldest and one of the most complete skulls that we can definitely assign to modern man – the race known as *Homo sapiens sapiens* to distinguish it from earlier races of *Homo sapiens*.

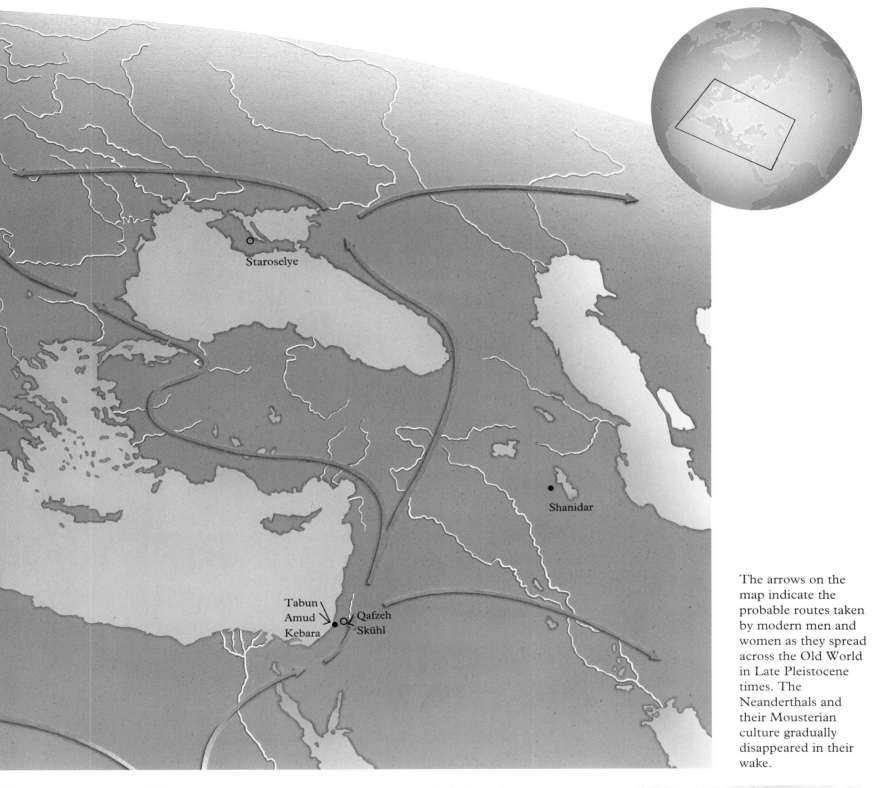

Staroselye

Shanidar

Tabun
Amud
Kebara

Qafzeh
Skūhl

The arrows on the map indicate the probable routes taken by modern men and women as they spread across the Old World in Late Pleistocene times. The Neanderthals and their Mousterian culture gradually disappeared in their wake.

11 THE SPREAD OF HOMO SAPIENS

The remains of Neanderthal settlements, found in many areas of Europe and Asia, show that the Neanderthals were good toolmakers and suggest that they had reached quite a high level of intelligence. Their practice of burying their dead suggests that they also had spiritual beliefs. But the Neanderthals and their Mousterian culture did not last. They disappeared completely about 35,000 years ago. It was once thought that the Neanderthals were killed by more modern people, belonging to our own species – *Homo sapiens sapiens* – who moved into the Neanderthals' territories at about that time, but it is much more likely that the Neanderthals died out gradually.

One thing that is certain is that modern people did not descend from the Neanderthals, because fossils discovered at Qafzeh, in Israel, show that people with quite modern features were already in existence about 90,000 years ago. These men and women were the descendants of one of the early races of *Homo sapiens* living in Africa, while the Neanderthals descended from a separate race of early or archaic people.

Tools and travel

From the Near East, modern men and women spread around the coasts of Europe and the Black Sea, and by about 30,000 years ago, were living in many parts of Europe and Asia. During Upper Palaeolithic times the people reached new levels of social behaviour and co-operation, and probably acquired new religious beliefs as well.

People certainly rose to new artistic levels, using the Levalloisian technique (see page 43) to fashion fine blades and many other small tools from flint. This new industry, known as leptolithic from the Greek words *leptos* (thin) and *lithos* (stone), gave the people much

A reconstruction of a Stone Age *Homo sapiens* from Late Palaeolithic times. He wore clothes made from animal skins and furs. The bow and arrow became an important weapon at about this time.

greater mobility. The hunters, in particular, could carry plentiful supplies of spear-heads and arrow-heads without being weighed down. They could travel further and spend more time actually hunting and fishing. Bows and arrows made hunting much easier, and fishing became much more efficient with the development of hooks and harpoons made of bone and horn. Fine stone tools were used to fashion these new weapons.

A group of modern men and women (pictured in colour on pages 44/45) marching across the tundra – the windswept land on the southern edge of the ice-cap that was still spreading across the northern parts of Eurasia in Late Palaeolithic times. They needed sturdy clothing, made from tanned hides and furs, to keep out the cold and the wet. Even their feet were covered, for the journey was long and arduous and the land was hard and rocky.

Their baggage consisted of bulky sacks, containing a little food but filled mainly with a good selection of points, knives, scrapers, and other stone cutting tools that could easily be fitted with handles when necessary.

On the journey, the men hunted wild game, which was then roasted over the fires that the people could light whenever they needed them. Some elk have been spotted in the valley on the right. Some are out of range, but one big male has reached the bank of the frozen lake. Two armed hunters approach cautiously, hiding themselves behind boulders and among the sparse bushes. The young man in the foreground holds a deadly new weapon – a spear-thrower that gives the spear much greater speed and power.

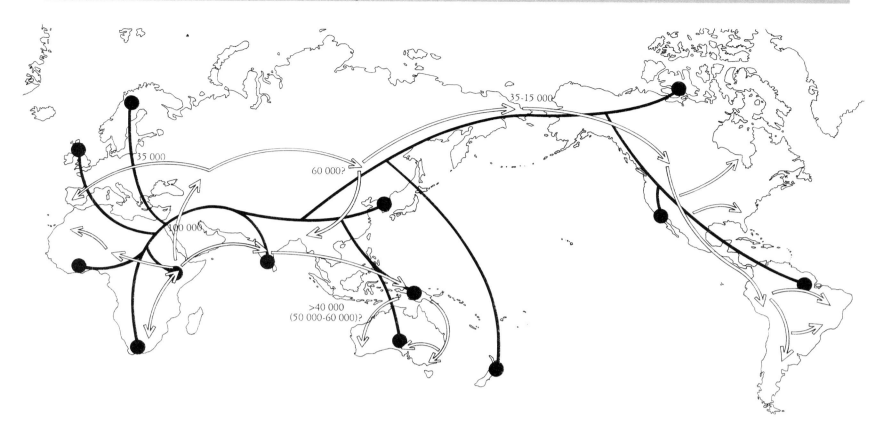

Possible migratory routes followed by *Homo sapiens* as they spread all over the world from their probable origin in East Africa. The dates indicate the oldest discoveries in each area while the black lines trace the origins of the various living races of people. Taken from L. Cavalli Sforza, *Genes, Peoples and Languages* in *Scientific American*, November 1991.

Religion and art

People's mental abilities were obviously developing quite quickly. Someone could 'see' an awl or an arrowhead in a still-shapeless lump of stone, and know exactly where to hit the lump to break off the new tool. They were able to modify tools for particular uses, and they were also taking the first steps towards figurative art.

The earliest traces of cave art are about 35,000 years old. At the same time people began making ornamental objects by engraving animal bones and teeth. The carvings may have expressed or represented ideas that were difficult to define, and so may have been a support for language – possibly the first attempts at writing!

The practice of burying the dead shows that people also had spiritual and religious beliefs. We cannot tell what they thought about death and what might happen after it, but the provision of food and weapons in graves shows that they believed that there was an afterlife.

With portable tools and fire at their disposal, modern men and women could move about freely and settle almost anywhere. Mobility was essential in Late Palaeolithic times, for the glaciers were still pushing southwards and forcing people to move out of their way.

Stone implements from Ksar Akil in Lebanon, dating from the beginning of the Upper Palaeolithic – the Late Old Stone Age – when the Mousterian culture was beginning to die out.
1 Levalloisian knife-point
2 Blade core from which blades are struck
3 Engraving tool for use on wood and bone
4 Scraper.

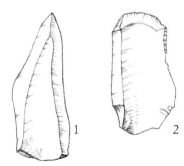  

12 STONE AGE ART IN WESTERN EUROPE

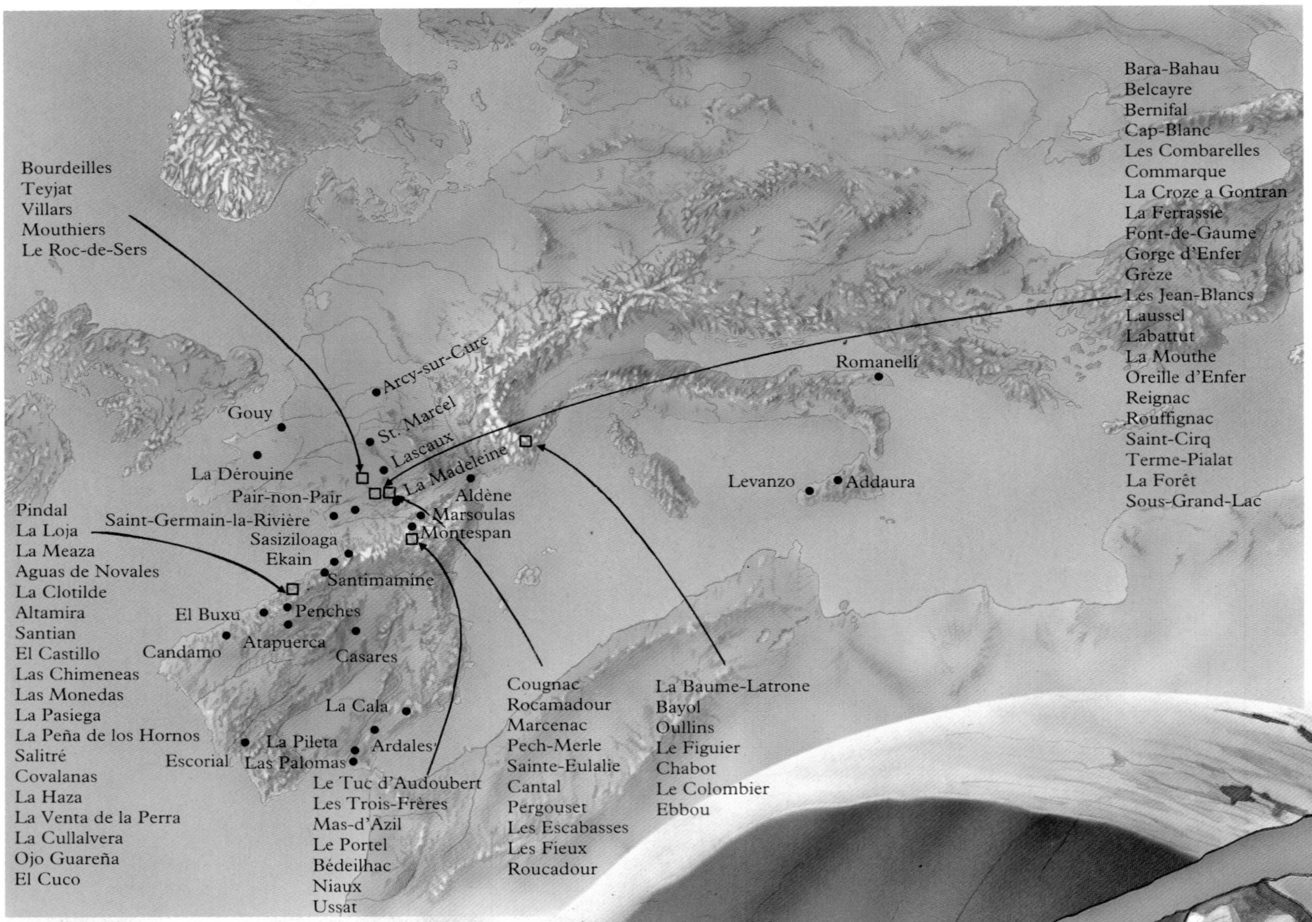

Bourdeilles
Teyjat
Villars
Mouthiers
Le Roc-de-Sers
Bara-Bahau
Belcayre
Bernifal
Cap-Blanc
Les Combarelles
Commarque
La Croze a Gontran
La Ferrassie
Font-de-Gaume
Gorge d'Enfer
Greze
Les Jean-Blancs
Laussel
Labattut
La Mouthe
Oreille d'Enfer
Reignac
Rouffignac
Saint-Cirq
Terme-Pialat
La Forêt
Sous-Grand-Lac
Romanelli
Arcy-sur-Cure
Gouy
St. Marcel
Lascaux
La Madeleine
La Dérouine
Pair-non-Pair
Aldène
Marsoulas
Montespan
Levanzo
Addaura
Saint-Germain-la-Rivière
Sasiziloaga
Ekain
Santimamine
Pindal
La Loja
La Meaza
Aguas de Novales
La Clotilde
Altamira
Santian
El Castillo
Las Chimeneas
Las Monedas
La Pasiega
La Peña de los Hornos
Salitré
Covalanas
La Haza
La Venta de la Perra
La Cullalvera
Ojo Guareña
El Cuco
El Buxu
Penches
Candamo
Atapuerca
Casares
La Cala
La Pileta
Ardales
Escorial
Las Palomas
Le Tuc d'Audoubert
Les Trois-Frères
Mas-d'Azil
Le Portel
Bédeilhac
Niaux
Ussat
Cougnac
Rocamadour
Marcenac
Pech-Merle
Sainte-Eulalie
Cantal
Pergouset
Les Escabasses
Les Fieux
Roucadour
La Baume-Latrone
Bayol
Oullins
Le Figuier
Chabot
Le Colombier
Ebbou

The major sites of cave paintings and engravings in Western Europe. The squares represent the centres of areas with many sites, the dots single finds.

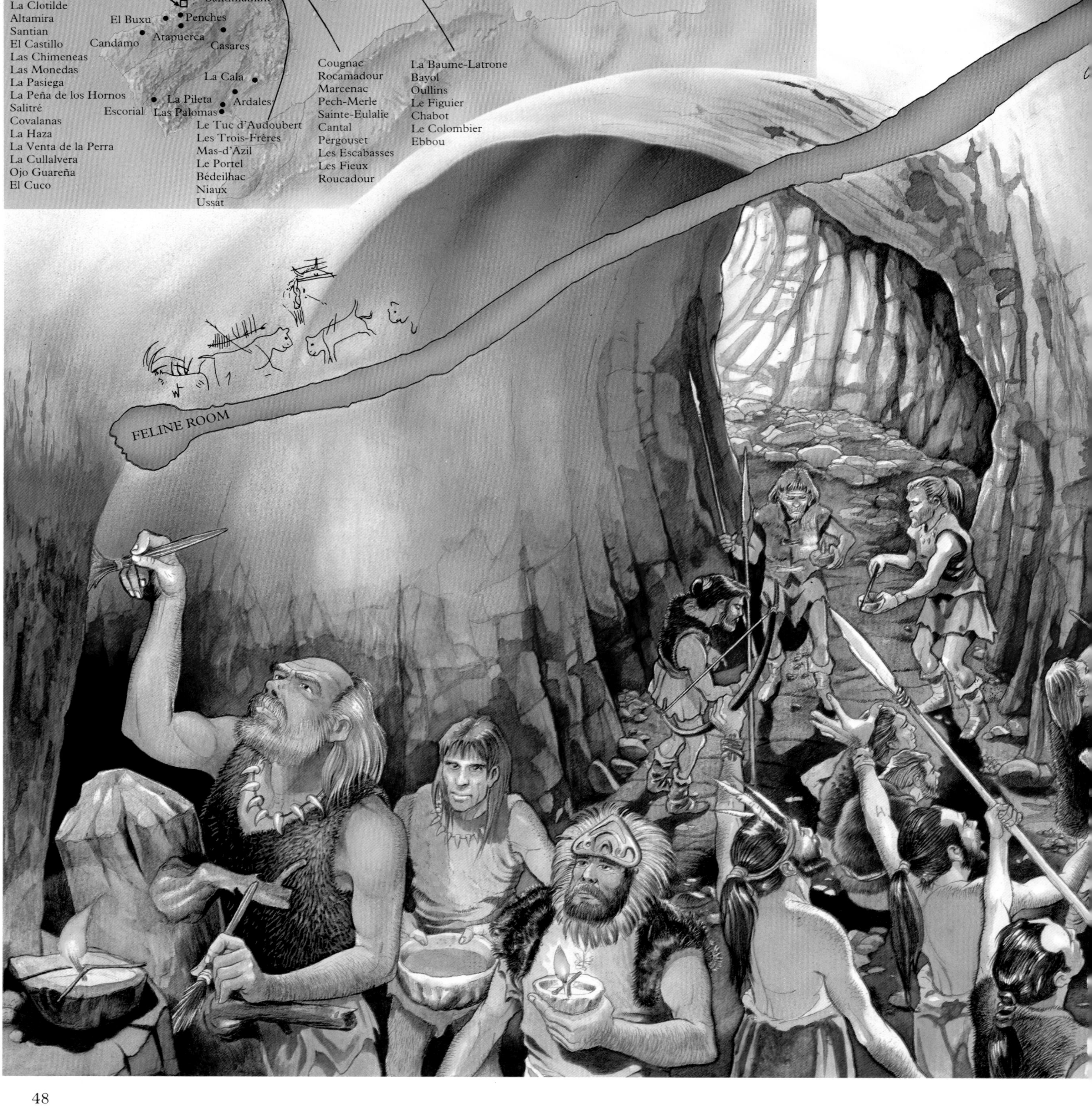

FELINE ROOM

The Lascaux cave, in the Dordogne region of France, was discovered by chance by two boys in 1940. It is up to 100m (328ft) deep and divided into several areas that are real 'exhibition rooms'. The Rotunda, or Hall of Bulls, contains a series of black and red paintings, including five huge bulls, which is the most monumental example of all Stone Age art.

More large cattle and deer decorate the Axial Gallery, together with curious signs in the form of crosses and trellises.

The least well-conserved area of the cave is the Passage, where the pictures are quite faded.

The Nave is decorated with four groups of horses, oxen, bison, and deer, while about 30 animals, including rhinos and deer, adorn the Feline Room.

The Apse is a small round room about 5m (16ft 6in) in diameter, at the bottom of which is a well.

APSE

NAVE

PASSAGE

ROTUNDA

AXIAL GALLERY

12 STONE AGE ART IN WESTERN EUROPE

Among the earliest of the truly modern human beings (*Homo sapiens sapiens*) in Europe were Cro-Magnon people, so-named because their remains were first found at Cro-Magnon in the Dordogne area of France. Cro-Magnons arrived about 30,000 years ago but, although they had some ancient features, they were anatomically well advanced and differed very little from today's human beings. They were quite tall – averaging about 1.7m (5ft 7in) – with long skulls, straight foreheads, prominent noses, and well-defined chins. Their culture is known as Aurignacian, from Aurignac in southern France where many of their tools were found, and is the oldest culture of Upper Palaeolithic times. It is characterized by small bone ornaments, delicate engraving tools and spear-heads made of stone.

Realism and stylization

The earliest forms of Stone Age art, in the form of simple carvings or engravings, also belong to the Aurignacian culture. Many of the carvings were of animals, but the figures were very stylized, with just a few conventional details making it possible for the animals to be identified. In a sense, these early pictures were nearer to writing than to art, but about 25,000 years ago the pictures began to get more realistic. The animals were then represented by clear outlines of the head and the back, with the addition of characteristic features for each species – horns for the bison, tusks for the mammoth, and a mane for the horse.

Human figures also began to appear, especially female ones in the form of statuettes carved from stone, bone, or ivory or made from fired clay. Known as 'Venuses', these statuettes did not show women in a realistic form. The breasts, buttocks, and hips were very

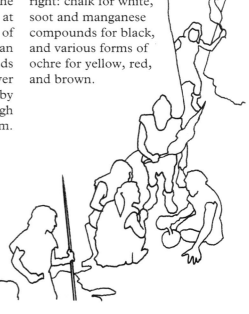

The map (opposite) shows the distribution of the world's major regions of rock art, including both paintings and engravings (source: E. Anati, *Rock Art Report to UNESCO*, 1984). There are about 780 regions, fairly evenly distributed over all the continents, and they contain thousands of individual sites with more than 20 million pictures or carvings. Among the countries that have made major contributions to the study and cataloguing of rock art are Australia, Canada, France, Mexico, Norway, the former Soviet Union, Spain, and Sweden.

This rock carving from Laussel, in the Dordogne region of France, depicts a woman holding a bison horn in her right hand (redrawn from the relief of A. Leroi-Gourhan). Carvings of this kind are characteristic of the Aurignacian culture that developed in Europe about 30,000 years ago.

exaggerated, while the head and limbs were much less obvious. It is thought that the statuettes were expressions of fertility and motherhood. They have been found in many parts of Europe.

A more highly evolved culture began to appear about 18,000 years ago. Called Solutrean, from Solutre in Central France, it was characterized by some extremely fine stone tools and weapons. These were produced by a new technique involving heating, which made the removal of fine flakes of flint by pressure much easier.

The scene (pictured in colour on pages 48/49) shows the inside of a cave where a group of hunters are painting the walls: perhaps it will become another sanctuary of prehistoric art. On the left, an artist has climbed nearly to the ceiling of the cave and is using a fur brush to trace the outline of a large animal that he wants to paint. A stone lamp filled with animal fat provides him with light.

Primitive ladders, made from tree trunks, are used to reach the highest parts of the walls and the ceiling. In the centre of the picture, right at the top of one of these ladders, an artist spreads the paint over the wall by blowing through a hollow stem.

The colours are prepared by two men sitting on the extreme right: chalk for white, soot and manganese compounds for black, and various forms of ochre for yellow, red, and brown.

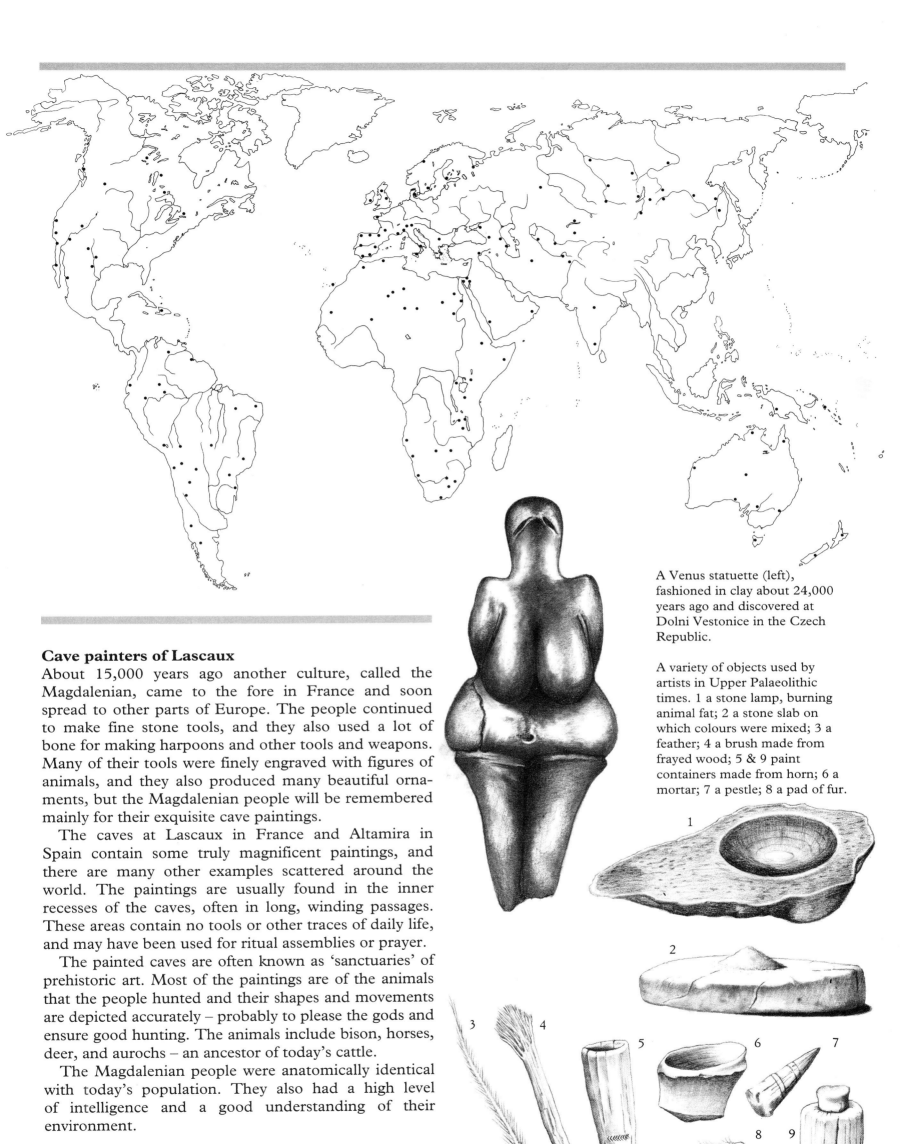

Cave painters of Lascaux

About 15,000 years ago another culture, called the Magdalenian, came to the fore in France and soon spread to other parts of Europe. The people continued to make fine stone tools, and they also used a lot of bone for making harpoons and other tools and weapons. Many of their tools were finely engraved with figures of animals, and they also produced many beautiful ornaments, but the Magdalenian people will be remembered mainly for their exquisite cave paintings.

The caves at Lascaux in France and Altamira in Spain contain some truly magnificent paintings, and there are many other examples scattered around the world. The paintings are usually found in the inner recesses of the caves, often in long, winding passages. These areas contain no tools or other traces of daily life, and may have been used for ritual assemblies or prayer.

The painted caves are often known as 'sanctuaries' of prehistoric art. Most of the paintings are of the animals that the people hunted and their shapes and movements are depicted accurately – probably to please the gods and ensure good hunting. The animals include bison, horses, deer, and aurochs – an ancestor of today's cattle.

The Magdalenian people were anatomically identical with today's population. They also had a high level of intelligence and a good understanding of their environment.

A Venus statuette (left), fashioned in clay about 24,000 years ago and discovered at Dolni Vestonice in the Czech Republic.

A variety of objects used by artists in Upper Palaeolithic times. 1 a stone lamp, burning animal fat; 2 a stone slab on which colours were mixed; 3 a feather; 4 a brush made from frayed wood; 5 & 9 paint containers made from horn; 6 a mortar; 7 a pestle; 8 a pad of fur.

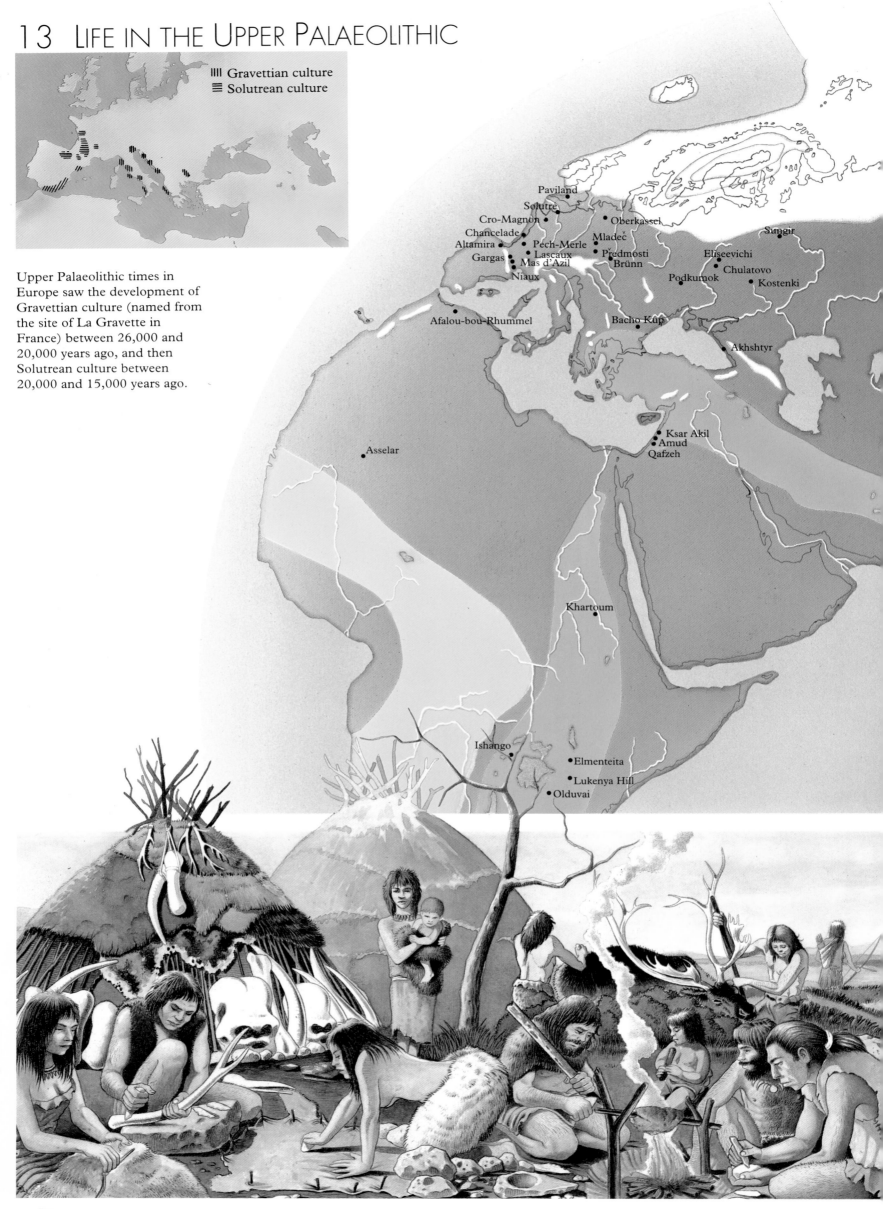

IIII Gravettian culture
☰ Solutrean culture

Upper Palaeolithic times in Europe saw the development of Gravettian culture (named from the site of La Gravette in France) between 26,000 and 20,000 years ago, and then Solutrean culture between 20,000 and 15,000 years ago.

Paviland
Solutré
Cro-Magnon
Oberkassel
Sungir
Chancelade
Mladeč
Altamira
Pech-Merle
Předmosti
Eliseevichi
Gargas
Lascaux
Brünn
Chulatovo
Mas d'Azil
Podkumok
Kostenki
Niaux

Afalou-bou-Rhummel
Bacho Kiro

Akhshtyr

Asselar
Ksar Akil
Amud
Qafzeh

Khartoum

Ishango
Elmenteita
Lukenya Hill
Olduvai

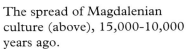

The spread of Magdalenian culture (above), 15,000–10,000 years ago.

Fatima Koba

Novoselovo • Mal'ta

Afontowa Gora

Choukoutien

Ordos

Minatogaa

Ziyang

Liujiang

Soan

Mahadaha

Hoa-Binh

Tabon Cave

Attirampakkam

Kota Tampan

Batadombalena

The large map shows the distribution of hunter-gatherer communities in the Upper Palaeolithic – the late Old Stone Age. The yellow areas are those most favourable to humans during periods of dry climate, and the red areas are those most favourable during periods of wetter climate.

13 Life in the Upper Palaeolithic

We now have a fairly accurate picture of what conditions were like in the Old Stone Age. We know that it was not cold and icy all the time. We also know that Stone-Age people did not always live in cold caves and leave them just to hunt animals for food. In reality, during the 25,000 years of the Upper Old Stone Age there were frequent climatic changes, with periods of intense cold alternating with much warmer periods.

Changing climates, changing vegetation

Just before the beginning of the last glacial period, about 35,000 years ago, Europe enjoyed a warm, moist climate that lasted for about 4,000 years. Pine and birch trees were dominant in Eastern and Central Europe, while most of Western Europe was covered with forests of oak, walnut, and alder. Wild oxen became more numerous than horses and reindeer became rarer. Wild boar and roe deer also lived in the forests. But the forests were gradually replaced in the less sheltered areas by grassy steppes that signalled a return to colder conditions and a new advance of the Würm glaciers. The land was swept by bitter winds, and the subsoil remained frozen all the year round. The reindeer again became the dominant animal in most parts of Europe.

About 30,000 years ago there was another warm spell, lasting for about 2,000 years, during which the Aurignacian culture spread over a large area of Europe. But then the climate became hostile again, with frozen tundra covering Central Europe and grassy steppes spreading over the eastern parts. Climatic changes of this kind had been going on throughout the Old Stone Age, and they continued until about 11,000 years ago, when things began to warm up again. The glaciers finally retreated from Europe about 8,000 years ago, with ice remaining in only a few mountainous regions.

From left to right: a Late Palaeolithic flute, made from a carved reindeer bone and found in Moldova near the Black Sea; a baton or command stick, probably used for straightening arrows and decorated with animal carvings; two throwing sticks, carved into animal shapes.

The improvement in the climate was accompanied by marked progress in toolmaking.

Hunter-gatherers

Modern humans (*Homo sapiens sapiens*) had already occupied most of the Old World and had made rapid advances in social and artistic fields as well as in toolmaking. They were hunter-gatherers, meaning that they gathered plant food as well as hunting animals. Both activities were determined by the natural resources of the environment, and there were no really permanent

The scene (pictured in colour on pages 52/53) is a plain in Western Europe towards the end of the Old Stone Age, about 15,000 years ago. A group of hunter-gatherers calmly go about their daily work in front of the village dwellings.

On the left, a woman uses a bone needle to sew up a cloak of reindeer skin, while her companion cuts a reindeer horn and a third woman removes the grease from another skin with a scraper.

In the centre, a hunter is carving a little statue from a fragment of bone, while his companions roast a small animal. Behind them, two young hunters are starting to skin a recently killed reindeer before cutting it up.

In the distance another hunter is about to use the latest invention – the bow and arrow – to kill a reindeer.

On the right, a mammoth has fallen into a trap. Wounded by repeated thrusts with the javelins, it will soon supply the community with abundant meat, clothing, and building materials.

The huts on the left are made from mammoth bones and wooden poles covered with reeds and the skins of large animals.

A possible way of using the baton stick to straighten an arrow.

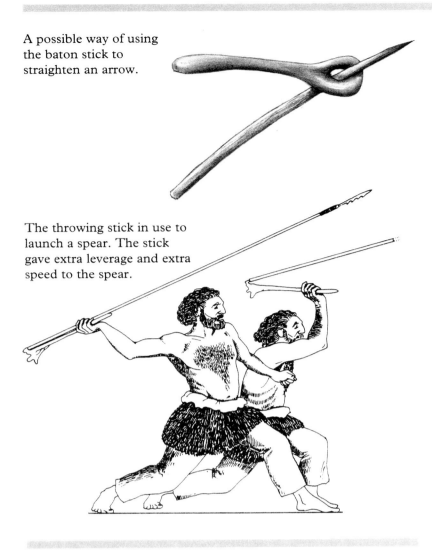

The throwing stick in use to launch a spear. The stick gave extra leverage and extra speed to the spear.

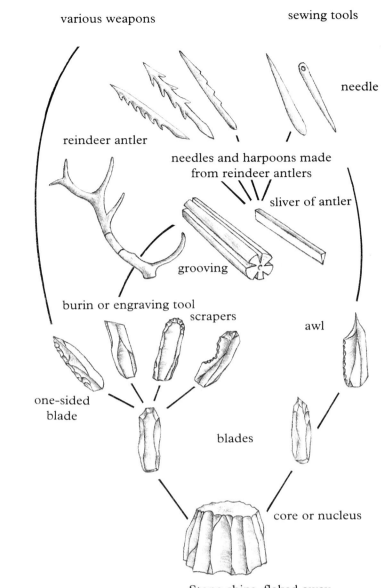

various weapons

sewing tools

needle

reindeer antler

needles and harpoons made from reindeer antlers

sliver of antler

grooving

burin or engraving tool

scrapers

awl

one-sided blade

blades

core or nucleus

Stone chips, flaked away from a simple core or nucleus, were worked in various ways to produce a range of tools which could then be used to fashion more specialized tools and weapons from wood and bone.

settlements during the Old Stone Age. People usually followed the grazing herds and moved with the seasons. Hunting took place in both warm and cold periods, but plant foods, mostly in the form of fruits and roots, were obviously more important during the warmer periods.

Hunting was carried out in groups, especially when attacking large prey, but towards the end of the Old Stone Age – the Upper Palaeolithic – hunters began to make much wider use of traps. These were large covered holes into which animals were driven so that they could be killed more easily. The bow and arrow, invented towards the end of the Old Stone Age, made hunting much more efficient, especially the hunting of medium-sized animals. It meant that the hunters did not have to get so close to their prey, so they did not frighten the animals or endanger themselves. A group of archers could even attack and kill a large mammoth.

Deer and other animals provided skins for clothes and antlers for making tools, as well as supplying plenty of meat. The great mammoths provided huge amounts of meat, and their ivory tusks had several uses: as well as being fashioned into weapons, many were carved into beautiful ornaments – and whole tusks and jaw bones were often used for building huts. People built huts in warm periods but often moved into caves during cold spells.

The artistic carvings and other remains, including properly buried bodies, show that people had a well-organized social life. They may have lived in 'clans', and neighbouring clans may have exchanged food and other materials. They may even have arranged marriages between men and women from different clans.

The Venus of Brassempouy – an ivory head found in the Landes region of France.

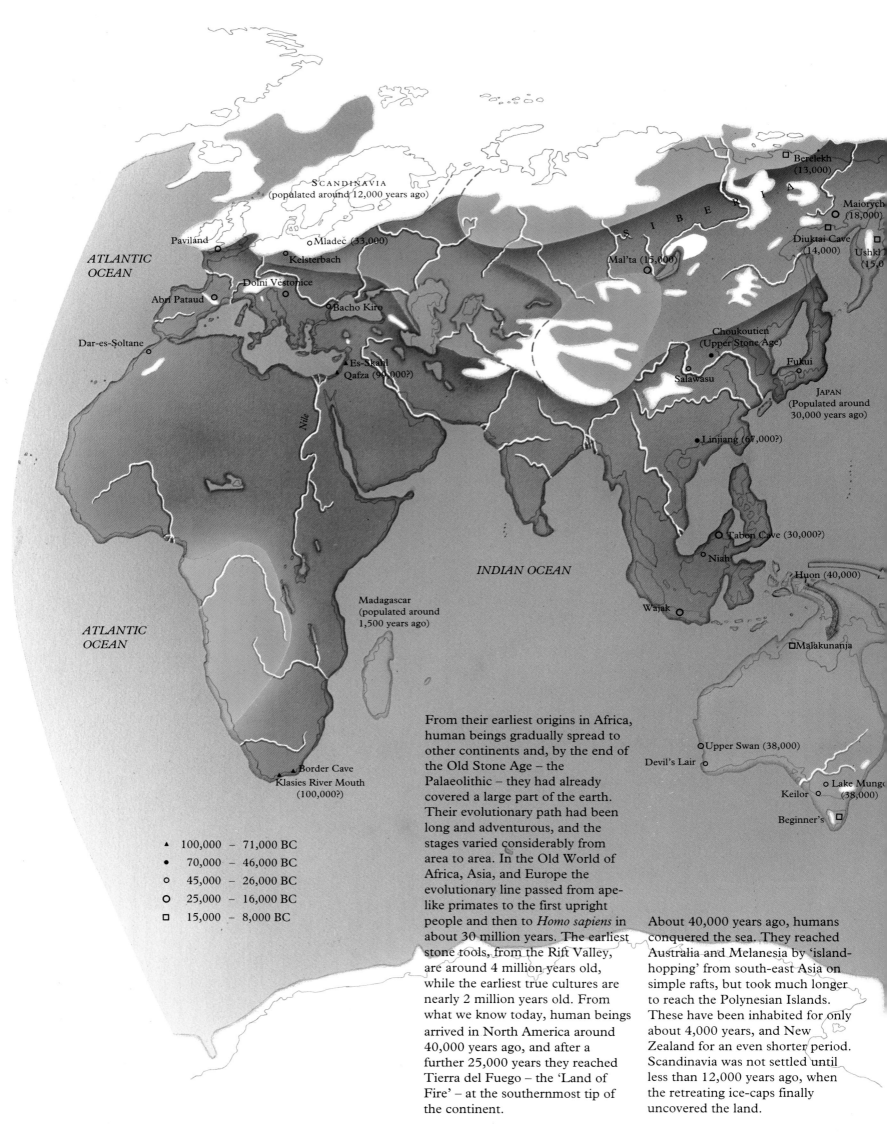

SCANDINAVIA
(populated around 12,000 years ago)

□ Berelekh
(13,000)

Maiorych
(18,000)

Diuktai Cave
(14,000)

Ushkl
(15,0

Paviland
Mladeč (33,000)

Kelsterbach

S I B E R I A

ATLANTIC
OCEAN

Dolni Věstonice

Abri Pataud

Bacho Kiro

Mal'ta (15,000)

Dar-es-Soltane

Choukoutien
(Upper Stone Age)

Fukui

Es-Skuhl
Qafza (90,000?)

Salawasu

JAPAN
(Populated around
30,000 years ago)

Nile

Linjiang (67,000?)

Tabon Cave (30,000?)

Niah

INDIAN OCEAN

Huon (40,000)

Madagascar
(populated around
1,500 years ago)

Wajak

ATLANTIC
OCEAN

□Malakunanja

▲ 100,000 – 71,000 BC
• 70,000 – 46,000 BC
○ 45,000 – 26,000 BC
◎ 25,000 – 16,000 BC
□ 15,000 – 8,000 BC

Border Cave
Klasies River Mouth
(100,000?)

Upper Swan (38,000)

Devil's Lair

Lake Mungo
(38,000)

Keilor

Beginner's

From their earliest origins in Africa, human beings gradually spread to other continents and, by the end of the Old Stone Age – the Palaeolithic – they had already covered a large part of the earth. Their evolutionary path had been long and adventurous, and the stages varied considerably from area to area. In the Old World of Africa, Asia, and Europe the evolutionary line passed from ape-like primates to the first upright people and then to *Homo sapiens* in about 30 million years. The earliest stone tools, from the Rift Valley, are around 4 million years old, while the earliest true cultures are nearly 2 million years old. From what we know today, human beings arrived in North America around 40,000 years ago, and after a further 25,000 years they reached Tierra del Fuego – the 'Land of Fire' – at the southernmost tip of the continent.

About 40,000 years ago, humans conquered the sea. They reached Australia and Melanesia by 'island-hopping' from south-east Asia on simple rafts, but took much longer to reach the Polynesian Islands. These have been inhabited for only about 4,000 years, and New Zealand for an even shorter period. Scandinavia was not settled until less than 12,000 years ago, when the retreating ice-caps finally uncovered the land.

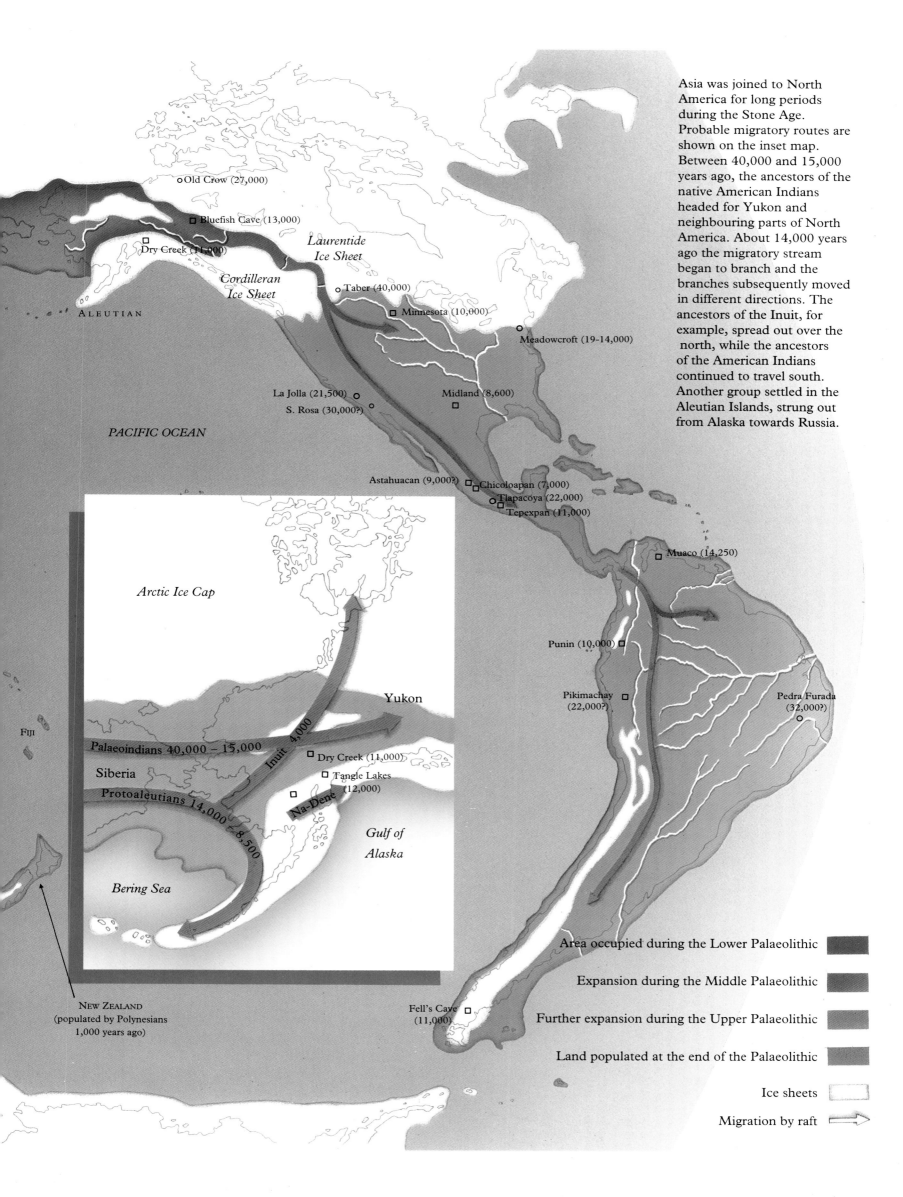

Old Crow (27,000)

Bluefish Cave (13,000)

Dry Creek (11,000)

Laurentide Ice Sheet

Cordilleran Ice Sheet

ALEUTIAN

Taber (40,000)

Minnesota (10,000)

Meadowcroft (19-14,000)

La Jolla (21,500)

S. Rosa (30,000?)

Midland (8,600)

PACIFIC OCEAN

Astahuacan (9,000?) Chicoloapan (7,000)

Tlapacoya (22,000)

Tepexpan (11,000)

Muaco (14,250)

Asia was joined to North America for long periods during the Stone Age. Probable migratory routes are shown on the inset map. Between 40,000 and 15,000 years ago, the ancestors of the native American Indians headed for Yukon and neighbouring parts of North America. About 14,000 years ago the migratory stream began to branch and the branches subsequently moved in different directions. The ancestors of the Inuit, for example, spread out over the north, while the ancestors of the American Indians continued to travel south. Another group settled in the Aleutian Islands, strung out from Alaska towards Russia.

Arctic Ice Cap

FIJI

Yukon

Palaeoindians 40,000 − 15,000

Inuit 4,000

Siberia

Protoaleutians 14,000 − 8,500

Dry Creek (11,000)

Tangle Lakes (12,000)

Na-Dene

Gulf of Alaska

Bering Sea

NEW ZEALAND (populated by Polynesians 1,000 years ago)

Punin (10,000)

Pikimachay (22,000?)

Pedra Furada (32,000?)

Fell's Cave (11,000)

Area occupied during the Lower Palaeolithic

Expansion during the Middle Palaeolithic

Further expansion during the Upper Palaeolithic

Land populated at the end of the Palaeolithic

Ice sheets

Migration by raft

14 Modern People Populate the World

The rapid physical and cultural evolution of human beings, the need to discover new hunting grounds, and perhaps simple curiosity about the surrounding lands, led people a long way from their African birthplace in a relatively short time. During Upper Palaeolithic times, major advances were made in technical, social, and artistic skills all over Europe and the Near East and right across the vast plains of Asia to China.

Social organization

Rare discoveries of the remains of huts and other shelters, at or below ground level, suggest that some settlements accommodated up to 200 people. We have no real proof of their social organization, but rock paintings and carvings of masked men dressed in animal skins indicate that these might have been 'priests' involved with religious or magical ceremonies. The 'priests' may have had a privileged position in the community, but the other members were probably all of the same social standing. Even the chief or head-man probably had no real power, other than deciding when and where to hunt.

There is, however, plenty of evidence for a division of labour within each community. The making of flint tools and other implements and weapons was probably carried out by older individuals – possibly men who were no longer able to hunt. The women probably did most of the chores, including preparing skins and sewing clothes, while the numerous paintings and engravings would have been the work of a few particularly talented individuals – just as in today's society.

From northern Asia to North America

The colonization of northern Asia began towards the end of the Palaeolithic and soon reached what is now the northern part of Mongolia. The people showed a high level of adaptation to the harsh climate. They specialized in hunting the mammoth and the woolly rhinoceros, making clothes from their fur and using their bones to build permanent huts or houses. They also made a wide range of delicate bone tools.

Some of the groups that populated Siberia gradually moved on to North America, crossing the land bridge, called Beringia, that joined eastern Asia to Alaska during the ice ages. The 'bridge' sank about 10,000 years ago, when the melting glaciers poured all their water back into the oceans. The first phase of immigration into Alaska took place over quite a long period between 70,000 and 35,000 years ago, and a second wave of immigrants crossed over between 28,000 and 10,000 years ago. Many animals, including the mammoth, the bison, and the horse, also made use of the land bridge.

Down to South America

From Alaska and neighbouring Yukon, people spread all over the American continent, moving southwards along a narrow corridor between the Cordilleran and

A rock painting (above) of a hunting scene, discovered near Castellon in eastern Spain, and (left) a figure called the 'witch doctor', discovered in the 'Cave of Three Brothers' in southwest France. It represents a creature that is half man and half beast.

Laurentide ice sheets. The stone tools they left behind show that there were people living in Canada 40,000 years ago, while discoveries at Tlapacoya show that they had reached Mexico at least 22,000 years ago. They continued to push southwards, and remains found at Lagoa Santa in Brazil show that people were living in South America over 10,000 years ago.

Crossing the sea

People reached Indonesia quite early on, although we do not know whether they arrived by land or by sea. Indonesia is now separated from the mainland of Asia by only a few kilometres of sea, and during the ice ages there may well have been dry land between the two. The remains of stone industries around Lake Mungo in Australia are thought to be about 35,000 years old, but people probably arrived in northern Australia much earlier than that – perhaps by sea or perhaps by means of a land bridge from Indonesia. A few Upper Pleistocene remains in Australia recall Solo Man (*Homo erectus*), who lived in Indonesia some 250,000 years ago and whose features had several similarities to the Aborigines living in Australia today.

The small maps (far right) show how the human population spread over the world during prehistoric times. The graph (right) shows how the estimated population increased gradually during the Old Stone Age and then shot up rapidly during the Middle and New Stone Ages between 10,000 and 6,000 years ago.

Gravettian tools:
1 & 2 Scrapers
3 Knife points
4 Small detachable knife blades (microliths) for use with wooden or bone handles
5 & 6 Hand-knives, with blunted back edges, from the Upper Gravettian culture of Spain

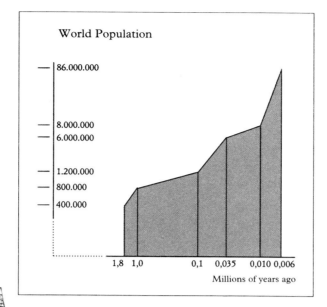

World Population

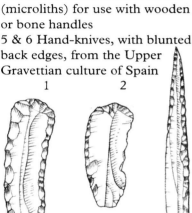

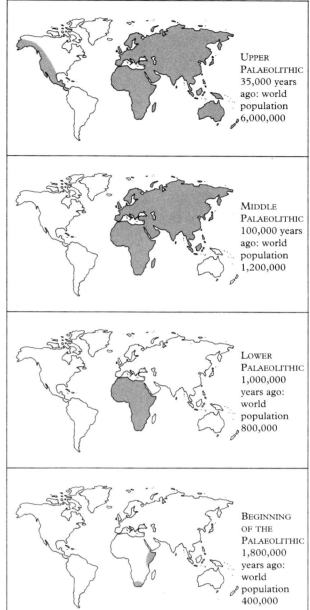

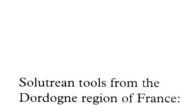

Solutrean tools from the Dordogne region of France:
1 & 2 Scrapers

3 & 4 Shouldered leaf-points
5 Flat-sided point

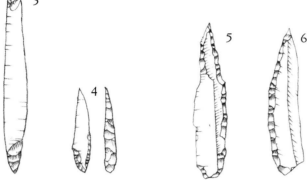

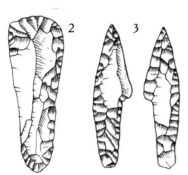

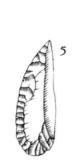

Magdalenian tools from the Dordogne region of France:
1-4 Needles and harpoons

5 Scraper
6 Burin or engraving tool
7 Awl

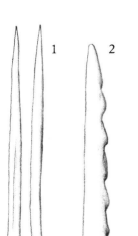

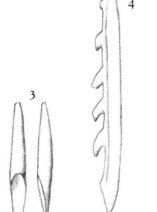

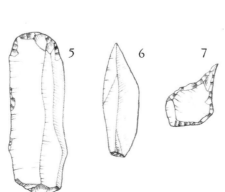

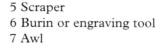

TECHNOLOGY IN THE UPPER PALAEOLITHIC
The *Chatelperronian* culture, which lasted from about 35,000 to 30,000 years ago, was characterized by knife blades that were straight and sharp on one edge and blunt and rounded on the other. There were also cylindrical points that were probably used to tip spears.

The *Aurignacian* culture, which lasted from about 30,000 to 27,000 years ago, produced simple rock carvings with a wide range of pointed engraving tools or burins. This culture was also characterized by stone or bone points that were notched at the base for fitting to hunting spears.

The *Gravettian* culture, which employed a wide range of slender knives and other cutting and scraping tools, also produced decorated batons or command sticks, made from bones or antlers.

About 20,000 years ago the *Solutrean* culture developed in Western Europe. The people used bone needles and a range of very thin and delicate stone blades, many of which were leaf-like and often notched or 'shouldered' on one side.

The *Magdalenian* culture appeared in Europe about 15,000 years ago, when bone-work reached its highest development. The Magdalenians made elaborate and highly-decorated harpoons and spear-throwers, but they will be remembered mostly for their beautiful cave paintings.

Glossary

Acheulean An early Palaeolithic culture, characterized by the use of roughly-shaped stone hand-axes that were often more or less triangular or almond-shaped. Named after Saint Acheul in France, where many such axes have been found.

Anthropoid Any member of the branch of primates that includes monkeys, apes, and people.

Aurignacian One of the earliest cultures of modern humans, appearing in Upper Palaeolithic times and exhibiting the earliest examples of art – in the form of engravings on rocks and cave walls. Named after Aurignac in France.

Australopithecine Name given to any of the early hominids – members of the human family – that still had many ape-like features although they walked more or less upright on two legs. Living in Africa as much as 5 million years ago, they are the oldest known members of the human family. The name means 'southern ape'.

Baton An implement, usually made from a reindeer antler, with one or more holes in it that was probably used for straightening spears and arrows. It was often beautifully carved. Also known as a command stick, it may have been a sign of authority.

Bifacial A description applied to any stone cutting tool that had been chipped or sharpened on both sides of the main blade.

Brachiation The method of locomotion used by gibbons and orangs, in which they swing from branch to branch with their arms.

Burin A pointed tool, made from stone and used for carving designs on cave walls or for engraving bones and antlers.

Chatelperronian A culture existing in Europe at the beginning of Upper Palaeolithic times from about 35,000 to 30,000 years ago. Named after Chatelperron in France.

Chip Any of the small pieces chipped away from a larger stone during toolmaking. Many of the chips were then worked on

and turned into smaller tools. Flattened chips are often called flakes.

Chopping tool Any large stone tool, often hand-sized, with a cutting edge produced by chipping or flaking from both sides.

Clactonian A stone or tool industry of Lower Palaeolithic times, characterized by roughly shaped cutting tools with very angular faces. Named after Clacton-on-Sea in England.

Core The original stone from which chips or flakes were removed to form tools. Also known as a nucleus.

Cranial capacity The size of the brain case of a skull, and therefore of the brain itself. It gradually increased during evolution as humans became more intelligent.

Cranium Another word for the skull, but especially the upper part that houses the brain.

Culture The sum total of all the knowledge, ideas, and material possessions of a particular society or civilization at a particular period of history.

Demographic Concerning the size, growth, and distribution of populations.

Epoch A name given to some of the smaller divisions of geological time, especially to the divisions of the Tertiary Period.

Era A name given to any of the major divisions of geological time, such as the Palaeozoic (ancient life) and Cenozoic (recent life) eras.

Evolution The gradual change of an animal or plant species from one form to another – usually into a more complex form. The word is also applied to the changing or advancing cultures of prehistoric people.

Find A name used for any discovery of fossils or other remains in the earth.

Flint A very hard but brittle rock, usually found in chalk deposits. It is easy to chip or flake to produce sharp cutting edges. Chert is another rock with similar properties.

Fossil The remains or traces of a plant or animal preserved in the rocks.

Genus One of the categories used in classifying living things. The members of a genus are all quite similar and closely related, and they share the same name. *Homo habilis, Homo erectus,* and *Homo sapiens* are all true human beings, belonging to the genus *Homo.* (See Species.)

Glaciation A time of great cold, during which ice sheets or glaciers spread over the land. There were several glaciations or ice ages during the Pleistocene Period, some of them lasting for many thousands of years.

Graffiti A general name given to the early forms of art, consisting of simple engravings on rocks or on pieces of wood and bone.

Gravettian A stone tool culture existing in Europe during Upper Palaeolithic times and characterized by a variety of small, pointed flint knife-blades.

Habitat The particular environment in which a plant or animal species lives.

Harpoon A sharply pointed and hooked weapon, thrown or fired at prey. When fastened to a line it was used for fishing. It was usually made from bone or antler, or else from small stone flakes fitted to a shaft of wood or bone.

Hominid Any member of the human family – the Hominidae.

Hominoid Any member of the superfamily Hominoidea, which includes apes as well as all fossil and living human beings.

Ice age Any of the various times during the earth's history when the climate became very cold and ice sheets or glaciers spread over large areas of the land and sea (see Glaciation). The sea level always fell during the ice ages, because so much water was locked up in the ice, and lands that are now separated by sea were often linked by dry land. The most recent ice age ended only about 10,000 years ago.

Interglacial A period of warmer and less harsh conditions between two glaciations.

Magdalenian An Upper Palaeolithic culture, characterized by very thin flint tools, beautifully carved antler tools and, above all, by magnificent cave-paintings. Existing until about 12,000 years ago, it was named after La Madeleine, in France, where many objects have been found.

Mesolithic The Middle Stone Age, beginning about 12,000 years ago in Europe and lasting for about 5,000 years. Most of the stone tools of this age were microliths – very small, replaceable blades and points fitted into bone or wooden handles.

Mobile art A name sometimes given to small, portable carved objects, such as statuettes, batons and throwing sticks.

Mousterian A Middle Palaeolithic culture particularly associated with Neanderthal people in Europe. The stone tools were made from relatively thick flakes of flint or chert and included a variety of scrapers and double-edged knives. In most areas there were also triangular or almond-shaped hand-axes. Named after Le Moustier in France.

Neanderthal An extinct species of people (*Homo neanderthalensis*) living mainly in Europe between about 100,000 and 35,000 years ago. They were rather heavily built and not the ancestors of modern people.

Neolithic The New Stone Age, beginning in Europe about 7,000 years ago. Stone tools were beginning to give way to metal ones, and the old hunting and gathering way of life gradually gave way to farming.

Nucleus See Core.

Ochre An iron-containing pigment, obtained from red or yellow clay and used for wall-painting.

Oldowan A Lower Palaeolithic culture, existing in East Africa as much as 1,750,000 years ago and characterized by crudely shaped, hand-sized chopping tools. It is also called Olduvian, from Olduvai Gorge in Tanzania.

Omnivorous Eating both plant and animal food.

Palaeolithic The Old Stone Age, beginning when people first started to make simple stone tools about 2,000,000 years ago and lasting until about 12,000 years ago.

Palaeontology The study of fossils.

Pangaea Name given to the single large mass of land that existed from the Permian Period until the Jurassic Period (from about 260 million years ago until about 200 million years ago) and then began to break up to form the continents that we know today.

Panidae A name sometimes used for the family containing the chimpanzee and gorilla, although these are more often included with the orang-utan in the Pongidae.

Percussion The method of removing a chip or flake from a stone core by hitting it with another object – usually another stone.

Period Any of the major divisions of geological time, such as the Cretaceous or Carboniferous.

Pleistocene The geological period, lasting from about 2,000,000 years ago until the end of the last ice age, a mere 10,000 years ago. This was the period during which most of human evolution took place.

Point Name given to any pointed stone tool used for cutting or engraving. Many were solid and pear-shaped, but some were leaf-like and often had notches on the sides.

Pongidae The family containing the great apes – the chimpanzee, gorilla, and the orang-utan. (See Panidae.)

Prehistoric Concerning that part of history dealing with life and culture before there were any written records.

Primates The group or order of mammals to which the monkeys, apes, and human beings belong. The two main branches are the anthropoids and the prosimians.

Prognathous Having a protruding jaw, a condition found in apes and many of the early hominids.

Prosimian Any member of the primitive branch of primates containing the lemurs, lorises, and tarsiers.

Rock art Name given to the wide range of engravings and paintings with which Stone-Age people decorated rocks and cave walls.

Savanna The tree-dotted grassy plain covering a large area of tropical Africa.

Sedimentary rock Any rock that has been formed, usually underwater, through the accumulation of sand, mud, and other material and then solidified. These rocks often contain fossils of animals that were living at the time they were formed. (See Volcanic rock.)

Solutrean An Upper Palaeolithic culture, existing in Europe between about 20,000 and 15,000 years ago. Characterized by thin blade-like tools produced by the skilful use of pressure on the edges of the blades, it is named after the prehistoric site of Solutre in France.

Species Each individual kind of plant or animal is called a species, and closely related species are grouped into a genus. Each species has a scientific name consisting of the name of its genus and a specific name. Modern people are *Homo sapiens*, a name which means 'wise member of the genus *Homo*'. Other human species include *Homo erectus* and *Homo neanderthalensis*.

Throwing stick A device, usually made of wood, for giving extra leverage and therefore extra speed and power to a spear when it is thrown.

Tundra The cold, windswept and treeless region around the edges of the Arctic Ocean. During the ice ages, when glaciers spread far to the south, the tundra was far to the south of its present position.

Volcanic rock Rock that solidified from molten lava, forced out through volcanoes or through other cracks in the earth's crust.

INDEX